First Church of the Brethren
1340 Forge Road
Carlisle, Pennsylvania 17013

A Pew for One, Please

A Pew for One, Please

The Church
and the Single Person

WILLIAM LYON

A CROSSROAD BOOK
The Seabury Press • New York

I wish to acknowledge the invaluable assistance of Ms. Arlene Roehm. In addition to conducting much of the research and evaluation, she contributed many useful suggestions and ideas embodied in this book. The need for this book was first recognized by my editor, William Gentz. Finishing the book was made possible by Edward Lohrbach, whose ranch provided a retreat.

I am grateful, also, for the forebearance and encouragement of my wife, Elizabeth, and the children: Belinda, Todd, Melody, Amy and Melissa.

William Lyon

1977
The Seabury Press
815 Second Avenue
New York, N.Y. 10017

Printed in the United States of America

Library of Congress Cataloging in Publication Data

Lyon, William, 1927-   A pew for one, please.
"A Crossroad book."
1. Church work with single people.   I. Title.
BV4437.L95   261.8'3   76-41976   ISBN 0-8164-0374-0

*To those who have loved and lost,
this book is dedicated as a reminder
that where God is, there Love is.*

Contents

Introduction

A Pew for One, Please

There are millions of Americans who are married, other millions who are single; millions of Americans attend church, while other millions do not. You fall into two of these categories and have been or will be in one or both of the other groups. This book, then, is about you.

Picture yourself entering a restaurant, alone. The hostess looks directly at you and, after waiting to see if you have a companion trailing behind, asks: "One?" You feel like saying "Don't rub it in," but instead answer, apologetically, "Yes."

"Right this way," she says, flashing her practiced smile of greeting. She doesn't remember you; there are so many customers coming and going. As you walk behind her on your way to the small table labeled "deuce" on her seating chart, you are conscious, self-conscious, of the flitting glances of the other diners. Are they wondering why you are alone? Feeling sorry for you? When you are seated, the hostess breaks contact by handing you a menu and ordering you to "enjoy your meal."

Your waitress sees you and quickly types you: "One: Maybe one cocktail at most. Probably wants to chat. Won't fuss about anything. Will finish and vacate the table quickly, 10 percent of one meal isn't much. Seen him before—always alone. Oh, well, I've been there myself, so I'll turn on my real friendly smile."

After she takes your order, you find yourself acutely aware of the conversation, the laughter, the interaction, the noise, which circulates around the room until it reaches you—a dead spot of silence and nonaction. Quickly you reach for the book or newspaper with which you had prepared yourself for this moment. You will probably continue to read—or pretend to—until you have hurriedly completed your meal and made your retreat.

In some churches, worshiping alone is not dissimilar to dining alone. Everyone is polite. They do the right things, like saying hello, showing you to a seat, offering you the day's program, even making available a Bible or songbook, which you can pretend to study. The result is the same: You feel welcomed, but not really welcome; acknowledged but not really known.

Other churches, which place a great store in being known as "a friendly church," operate more like cruise ships in their efforts to please and serve the newcomer. There is the head man known as the chief purser. He is flanked by his helpers, the assistant pursers. It is their job to corral a group of passengers and weld them into a friendly unit that, because its members will see so much of one another, will come to feel that it is a part of the larger group. The pursers have been trained to function as big brothers, social directors, and pom-pom boys exhorting one and all to keep busy, have fun, and above all, consider themselves part of the family. You will play deck games, exchange family photos, keep very busy, trade addresses with the invitation to "be sure and stop in if you're ever in the area," and return to home port. You never got to know the chief purser, you may never see the ship or its passengers again, but you did pass some time and have some fun.

The "cruise ship" churches and their singles programs are often very successful in a statistical sense: they are "booked" to capacity, although the passenger list is constantly changing. They sail frequently and make good time, yet few aboard know the destination.

Single people often join political clubs in the hopes of meeting a special person or, perhaps, hoping to get involved in something besides themselves. Should they pledge their fealty to an aspirant to the title of "Friend and Protector of the People," they may find themselves caught up in a demanding and exciting campaign. They will work tirelessly and selflessly for their leader, whose virtues and promises make him an omnipresent influence in their lives. A common zeal and purpose bind worker to co-worker. There develops a preoccupation and a sense of urgency about "the day." No effort must be spared, no shirking can be permitted if one is to share in the rewards of the "victory." Other interests, other acquaintances, dim in importance; for what can compare with the excitement of being part of a crusade? Who can compete with "the leader"? He appreciates and needs you, your co-workers respect and accept you. As long as there is a campaign to be fought and a cause to dedicate yourself to, you need not feel unwanted and unloved.

I have visited church singles groups whose members and leaders were so committed to doctrinal beliefs that they could tolerate no newcomer who could not or would not quickly accept the platform, join the party, and renounce their previous beliefs. In return, they will be given a secure future, a meaningful existence, a close-knit circle of acquaintances, and a new excitement. In short they will never again have to feel themselves alone.

There is another group, a group composed of individuals who, with one another, are able to dare, share, and care. They dare to reveal themselves as they really are, they share their hopes and fears about what is to come, they care about one another in the way that only people who trust each other can care. They may call themselves a prayer group, a therapy group, an alcoholics anonymous group, a koinonia group, a singles group, or a family. What matters is that they believe in one another and also in something greater than themselves. The single person who can find and commit himself to such a group will find friends, himself, and, perhaps, God.

There are churches, and programs within churches, that

are providing the kinds of practical, emotional, interpersonal, and spiritual support particularly needed by the unmarried person. This is not to say that the single person is necessarily lonely and insecure, but it is true that the single person can often use help either in escaping singleness or in adjusting to it. The church has always presented itself as the place where people could turn when they were troubled. This book will explore the questions of:

1. What is the church doing for the single person?
2. What *should* the church be doing for the single person?
3. How can the church better serve the single person and also fulfill its mission?

A Pew for One,
Please

1

The "Invisible" Single Person

In August of 1976, the *Los Angeles Times* indicated that there are 47 million single men and women in America, and that 12 million of them live alone. The others live with family, children, or male or female roommates. In California there are almost a million women living alone.[1] Singles are young, old, and in between. While there are more than 21 million persons over sixty years of age, one out of every six women over twenty-one is a widow.[2] While only 8 percent of the population will never marry, a progressively higher proportion alternate between being single and being married. For some time retailers and politicians have capitalized on a fact of life that the church has been slow, even reluctant, to accept: That single persons are—numerically, financially, and politically—a potent force. Whereas our political, commercial, and educational institutions have devoted a steadily increasing flow of their resources toward the single person, the church has continued to pretend that single persons constitute a small minority. Writing in the *Christian Ministry*, Doctor Otis Young of the First Congregational Church of Lincoln, Nebraska, stated that, "The church I serve discovered that one-fourth of all our members over the age of eighteen are single for whatever reason, and that more women than men are single, largely because of the number of widows in our midst."[3] In the same issue of *Christian Ministry*, Morgan Simmons, a staff member of Fourth Presbyterian church in Chicago, stated that, "When a church of 2,800 finds that at least 1,820 of its members are single, and that within ten blocks of its buildings 20,000 people make their homes, it has a special ministry to perform. . . . This ministry to singles extends over a fifty-year period, but its place in the life of the city is more needed today than ever. More and more young people are postponing or foregoing marriage, singles in larger numbers are leaving home with the hope of making it on their own; and there is an increasing number of divorces. They represent largely a group for whom urban living offers an alternate style of life. Although many singles live in close proximity to the church, many who participate in its programs come from the singles complexes located outside of the city and from suburban areas primarily oriented toward family activities."[4] Upon analyzing the church involvement of the single person participating in his church's singles programs, Simmons concluded that, "There are basically three types . . . those who have a deep interest in the church and a religious life; those who are neutral regarding the church; and there are those who have no church affiliation and who may even be antichurch. The largest majority fall into the first two categories."[5]

An interesting example of illogic can be illustrated by the following bit of reasoning:

1. Fact: Not many single persons attend church regularly.
2. Fact: Most people who attend church are members of a family.
3. Conclusion: The church should concentrate its efforts on families.

To say that churches in America are not only family-oriented but that they generally reject or ignore the single person is to state not an opinion but a fact. At one point in his article, Otis Young admits that "I didn't realize it until now, but most churches are 'couple oriented.' "[6] An Orange, California, clergyman, who organized a church aimed almost exclusively at single people, argues that: "Traditionally, churches don't know what to do with singles and unmarried people. The person who needs help comes away feeling like an outcast and often leaves the church altogether. . . . Churches," he believes, "have been losing ground for years because they haven't kept up with social needs."[7]

A needed change in attitudes toward single persons is declared by a Texas clergyman, "The vision of the church today needs to be enlarged to include the single adult on the church's new frontier."[8] Elmer Towns, who wrote one of the very few books written to date on the subject of the relationship between the single person and the church, justifies his own early work in developing young singles groups when he explains that "The average church program is oriented to the family. The family pew, the family picnic, and family altar have long been employed by the church. Now many churches are calling their Wednesday night Bible study and prayer meeting 'family night.' The emphasis on the family is needed, and nothing should be taken away from this emphasis. However, the young adult is lost in the struggle and as a result is neglected."[9] That anyone interested in building church-related young singles programs has his work cut out for him is suggested by the results of a 1971 poll, which showed that two-thirds of students rejected organized religion as an important value in a person's life, an increase of 7 percent since 1969.[10]

Although later in this book I will take issue with some of her statements, I am in full agreement with author Sarah Jepson's opinion when she asks, "Why has the church lost its concern for this sizable subculture, or did it ever have one? Are single adults so sophisticated and complex that they cannot be reached? Is it because their mobility rate (40 percent change residence each year) is so incredible that the church cannot keep up? Or can it be that the church has been too complacent in its traditional program of Sunday School, missionary societies, and worship services to innovate a vital program for this prime target group?"[11]

So far in this book there have been eleven references to books and articles on the subject of the single person and the church. Those who flinch at the prospect of plodding through literary references need have no fear for, with the exception of a few magazine and newspaper articles, an extensive library search of publications dealing with this subject in the past ten years unearthed only two or three books that could be considered as concentrating on this subject. It appears to be a common misconception that single persons comprise an insignificant minority. Few seem to realize that the various subgroups of single persons add up to a sizable number, perhaps a majority.

When a single person becomes a member of some group, he usually loses his identity as a "single." "Parents without Partners" are thought of as just that. "Senior citizens" groups have begun to forge both an identity and a reputation as a political and economic force to be reckoned with. But when we think of an elderly person, we usually think of him or her as a senior citizen rather than as a "single." An unmarried person is a bachelor or widow or divorcée or some other term that describes what he or she is *not*: married. Prejudice, and discrimination against the single person, have been so much a part of our culture that we look surprised, and innocent, when we are asked to consider how our income tax laws, housing regulations, banking policies, credit card rules, and employment policies discriminate against the single person. Harmful and unfair as such policies are, at least they are obvious and are based presumably on objective factors. More insidious and difficult to refute—because they are denied—are the beliefs that determine how our social institutions treat the single person.

When we analyze the relationship between the church and the single person, we must differentiate between church administration and church members. Historically, the Christian church has been devoted to the saving of individual souls. Our early leaders, including the Apostles and Disciples, either were, or became, single persons. Certainly, the single life was recommended as a preferred status for one who would lead a Christian life. St. Paul, in particular, declared that the single state is a gift from God. Even today, in many churches there is the attitude that one should give up the single state only in order to provide souls for Christ and members for the church; and should one be widowed or divorced, it is assumed that one will leave well enough alone. It is easy to understand why a pastor would rather enroll a married person in preference to a single person. The former will probably bring one or several of his family along as new members. They will, he knows, probably contribute more, for a longer period of time, than will a single person. The pastor wants to save individual souls, but he also has a church to run.

Church members themselves are often influenced by their own unacknowledged attitudes and beliefs regarding single people. The following are some thoughts and feelings that I have found among married church members:

"Single people don't stay around too long."

"Single people don't contribute much time or energy to the church."

"When I meet someone in their thirties or forties who hasn't been married, I can't help but wonder if they are homosexual."

"Jesus said that divorce is unacceptable. How can I then accept a divorced person's joining my church?"

"I don't know what to say to an old person; they don't seem to fit in unless they are married."

"Young, unmarried people are just interested in having fun. They aren't serious about religion."

"I think a lot of us are uneasy around unmarried members. We wonder if there is something wrong with them. Besides, they don't have the same interests as we do."

"Frankly, I don't like to associate closely with divorced people. I don't trust the women around my husband, and I'm afraid the men will put ideas into his head."

"I don't have anything against single people, but it's awk-ward trying to fit them into social functions or to exchange social visits with them. Our church is very family-oriented."

I believe that most pastors and parishoners are, at worst, prejudiced, or, at best, unconcerned about the spiritual and psychological needs of the single person. My opinion is based on what they do, not what they say. I believe, however, that much of this coldness is based more on ignorance than on meanness. Today's churches simply are not structured to pro-vide or encourage warm, interpersonal relationships in its approach to outsiders or even toward its own members. "It appears to be like a machine that is interested more in keep-ing moving and keeping its gears oiled than in developing spiritual insight and experience in the lives of its members. . . . Too often, in the impersonal established church the indi-vidual feels unwanted, rejected, alienated."[12]

If our churches characteristically cause, or allow, their members and visitors to feel unwanted, rejected, and alien-ated, it is not because they do not care. It is because our size, pace, and style of life are more dedicated to efficiency and growth than to intimacy and reflection. Samuel Beckett has said that: "One does not have to look for distress; it is scream-ing at you." In our flurry of activities and programs, we often do not hear the screams—or the silences. The history of minority groups and those not in power is that in order to im-prove their status they bind themselves together as a means of achieving recognition and change. Single people are only now beginning to create an identity as a group of individuals with unique needs.

I remember my own experience when, as a twenty-eight-year-old unmarried stranger, I visited a large church in the community to which I had recently moved. I had found the sermon inspiring and the music beautiful. When the minister invited everyone to attend the coffee hour following the ser-vice, I eagerly accepted. When I entered the social hall I was immediately greeted by the chief hostess, who gave me a quick, friendly smile and turned me over to the lady who was obviously assigned to taking care of visitors. Five minutes later, I felt like I had been in the company of the chairwoman of the religious welcome wagon. She did not learn much about me, but my head was filled with details of the multiplicity of activities to be found in her church. As she listed all that this church offered its members, I listened in vain for some clue as to where I might fit in. It seems that I was at an awkward age and status: I was not married, had no children, and there was no age group club into which I could fit. I considered saying that a hard life had taken its toll and that I only looked twenty-eight, but actually was eighteen. Or perhaps I could say that I was married and that my wife was visiting her mother for a few years.

I was passed on to the associate minister, whose warm, sincere manner did not keep me from feeling that I was being evaluated in terms of my potential usefulness to the church. I was then introduced to the leaders of the stewardship committee, the youth group, and the Fisherman (the ambulatory elderly). By the time I had agreed to give talks on Psychology and Growing Old, Psychology and Youth, Psychology and Marriage, Psychology and/or St. Paul, I had consumed five cups of coffee, twelve cookies, and one hour. Because of the pastor's brilliance and wisdom, and in spite of my status of single person, I attended the church for some years. I made friends, participated in church activities, and never felt at home. I never felt that anyone was at fault; I just didn't fit in.

My experiences as a church-attending single were not unique—as I learned during thousands of psychotherapy sessions with single people. Time and again I am asked, "Where *can* I go to meet some nice people? I don't meet anyone interesting at work, and I will not hang around bars!"

Divorced people complain that they feel like a third wheel, that their friends either avoid them or don't seem to know what to do with them. Sooner or later, the divorced person begins to consider dating and eventual remarriage and, whether or not he or she is a church attender, the divorced man or woman eventually considers the church as a possible center for meeting new people and making new friends. With rare exceptions, they come away disappointed. It seems odd that so many people should come to a common place in hopes of meeting each other, and fail to do so. Tragically, many of these lonely people forsake the church, unfulfilled emotionally—and spiritually.

The church has always been the haven to which people turn when they are in need. In the past few decades, most of the church's traditional helping functions have been taken over by social-political agencies and specialists. Except in rural communities, today's churches are usually centers of social interaction. For the single person in particular, the church has become a place that one visits at a certain time on a certain day (9:30 or 11 A.M. on Sunday) and becomes an anonymous participant in a group experience. For the single person, attendance at many church-related activities can be an unsatisfying, even painful experience. The following is an interview that I conducted with a woman we shall call Barbara. She is thirty-one, has been divorced for one year, has two small children, and is an executive secretary. She is bright, articulate, and charming, pretty—although slightly overweight—and very lonely.

Lyon: You mentioned to me that you no longer attend church services regularly; this in spite of the fact that you had been very involved in the church since childhood. Could you tell me why you've broken this lifetime pattern, or commitment, and how you feel about it?

Barbara: I'm not really sure what happened, myself. My husband and I both were really involved in our church. We put a lot into it, and we got a lot out of it. But then, when we separated and later divorced, people at the church went through a funny—no, not funny—a strange series of reactions.

Lyon: Strange reactions?

Barbara: Yes, at first everybody acted shocked—like they couldn't believe that Jim and I had had troubles all this time, or that it could be so bad that we would actually get divorced. After that, everybody seemed to feel sorry for me! Poor Barbara, to think that her husband left her with two children, and she's had to go to work—poor Barbara! Some of my women acquaintances seemed uneasy around me—like I was contagious. Some of the husbands acted the same way, and a few of them conveyed their willingness to brighten up my lonely evenings. I just couldn't take it; I wasn't the same person to them as I had been when I was married. I know that there were other single men and women in our church, but we've just never seemed to make contact. I became very self-conscious, so I quit going to church. I miss it, a lot."

Barbara's story is very different from Diane's. When I asked her why she had chosen the church she now attends, she replied: "Well, it was easy; I didn't have to shop around for a church. I had heard that this church had a singles program, so I got up my nerve and attended one of their meetings. At first, when I got there, I wished I hadn't come. But everyone was so friendly, and a couple of people talked to me a lot—they seemed really interested in me—and they had so many interesting things you could do that, well, before I knew it I was busy. They didn't rub my nose in it, but the officers and minister made it clear that this was a church-sponsored group and that religion was a basic part of their program. I liked that; if I hadn't I would have joined a ski club or gone somewhere else to meet people. This is what I wanted: to be able to have my social life related to my religious life. If and when I remarry, I'll stay in this church."

Barbara's and Diane's experiences as single persons in a church were very different. One woman felt that the church had failed her, so she left it. The other woman encountered the kinds of attitudes and programs that satisfied her emotional and spiritual needs. This book is intended to assist the reader in developing church-related singles programs that will put single people more in touch with themselves, with each other, and with God.

2

The Silenced Majority

If you are an unmarried Navajo woman of the Mormon faith, and also a physically disabled veteran who used to be an alcoholic and now are unemployed, you qualify for membership in seven separate minority groups. If you've counted, then you are wondering—why not eight? The answer is that if you are a single person, you are a member of a majority composed of such diverse groups as children, the elderly, the divorced, the homosexual, the widowed, the bachelor men and women, and the members of religious orders. And yet, in terms of visibility, organization, and success in improving their own lot, single people are treated, and seem to consider themselves as, an insignificant group of insignificant persons.

There are several reasons why single persons have not become the single people:

1. Single persons often consider their single status to be a temporary condition.
2. Many do not choose to be single: they are divorced, widowed, or have not "met the right person."
3. They do not have any great power as a group—as is evidenced by the discrimination employed against them by political bodies.

4. There is a subtle, but very real, social stigma attached to being a single person.
5. Single persons have not in the past had organizations that would bring them together.
6. Single persons suffer from an inferiority complex, which makes them reluctant to bring attention to themselves.
7. Their mobility makes it difficult for them to create and carry out plans for action.
8. Many are also members of other minority groups, to which they feel a primary identification and allegiance.
9. They have received very little encouragement or assistance from other power groups.

The results of the near invisibility of millions of single persons are many, and they are costly to those involved. But the picture is not all bleak. Single persons *are* doing something for themselves, and they *are* receiving help—especially from the churches. Before looking at a sample of what is being done for and by single persons in this country, we should specify which segment of the total singles population we wish to study, and which aspects of "the singles problem" interest us here.

One of the common mistakes of social service planners is to overgeneralize about the population group that they are studying. With reference to single persons in particular, it would be a gross error to assume that otherwise heterogeneous groups are made homogeneous by virtue of their sharing the one characteristic of being, for a time at least, unmarried. A nineteen-year-old college student's present life situation, and his hopes and plans for the future, differ from the present and future of a sixty-eight-year-old widow. There are many other assumptions that we must be cautious about making. For example, many unmarried persons are not really single (alone). There are hundreds of thousands of heterosexual and homosexual people who love and live together without being legally married to each other. Millions of other single persons live at home with their parents.

It is a common misconception that people become single persons because of some unlucky accident of fate—such as divorce, death, or age, or because no one wants them. And the state of being single is usually thought of as a condition that the single person will "cure" as soon as possible. When a person of twenty to forty says that he or she is single, we usually assume that he is "getting his need for a fling out of his system," that he is recuperating from a shipwrecked marriage in order to launch himself again, as soon as possible, on the sea of matrimony, or that he is some kind of celibate religious fanatic. It never seems to occur to others that some single persons are unmarried simply because they want to be unmarried—whether for awhile or forever—and, our culture is more tolerant of the single state among men than among women. A man who has never married is a bachelor. A woman who has not been married is labeled a "spinster" or, worse, "an old maid." Even so, nowadays we hear people coming right out into the open and declaring that they do not intend ever to marry—these are our former "closet singles."

There is no question about it, single persons are becoming more numerous and more conspicious. The trend toward later marriages among young people, the rising divorce rate (now over 40 percent), the willingness to identify oneself as a homosexual, the percentage of women surviving their husbands, the declining influence of the church in fostering marriages and preventing divorces (5 million American Catholics are divorced), the improved legal, financial, and social status of single women, "the new morality" (or should it be "the new immorality"?), and a new wave of assertiveness by minority groups have all combined to forge single persons into singles groups.

Singles groups are only now starting to marshall their resources and launch campaigns to dignify and fortify their position. New groups, programs, agencies, and information centers are spreading the word: The singles are here; they expect to be heard. And they are in touch with each other. Many clearing houses for singles news have been created, including such newsletters as *Single i* of Escondido, California, *Singles' Together* of Alhambra, California, and *Solo*, a magazine published by the Garden Grove Community Church of Garden Grove, California.

Church members all over the country are founding organizations devoted to single persons and their needs. In Salem, Oregon, The Oregon Christian Unmarried Adults offer social activities, information, and religious programs. Methodist churches in California are offering a steady stream of retreats and workshops. In Riverside, California, a Full Gospel Singles group meets bimonthly. Illinois is the family state for a national Born Again Singles in Christ (BASIC). West Virginia offers the Single Christians' National Association. In Mississippi there is the Christian Fellowship for Single Adults. The numbers grow. They vary in quality and effectiveness, but they are indicative of the newly found confidence and assertiveness of single persons.

It is too early to be certain, but it appears that the singles group that is most active and that is receiving the most attention is to be found in the age group between twenty-one and forty. The world of commerce is pouring millions of dollars into projects for attracting the singles' dollars. For example, here is the text of a circular that was left on my windshield this morning:

> Introducing a Christian
> Restaurant and Discoteque
> Light dinners served from 7 P.M. . . . with Sacred Music
> Dancing from 8 P.M. to midnight
> No alcoholic beverages, no smoking
> The atmosphere you've waited for

There are singles ski clubs, travel clubs, apartment houses, vacation resorts, golf and tennis tours—and those flourishing discotheques and key clubs where people at least pretend to be unmarried. Single persons in their twenties and thirties are the prime target, not only of the entrepreneurs, but of those churches who are expanding their ministry to previously unidentified clients. Magazines and newspapers from coast to coast run feature stories describing the personalities and life-styles of single persons. Such interviews usually take the form either of "How to survive while looking for Mr. or Ms. Right," or of apologies for the single life.

Within a three-month period, both the *New York Times* and the *Los Angeles Times* gave extensive coverage to single persons and singles groups. Both reports featured interviews with single persons who are not at all sure that they wish to marry or, more often, remarry. Because they illustrate a fact that is often unrecognized, that many single persons intend to remain single, I quote the following excerpts from both newspaper articles:

> Who needs it—this running around to find someone? I have all the closeness I need with other men. With a man you can say, "I don't want to see you tomorrow." With a woman, she gets upset. Who needs it?

> I'm a single woman, and I love it. I'll never get married again. I love my freedom. I want to belong to myself.

> What I want to know is, how do you have all that closeness, and then it ends? That's what I want to know.[1]

The Los Angeles newspaper feature story was titled, "They Want to Be Alone: Coping and Enjoying It." In it, relates the article, a woman psychologist states that:

> she finds, as do many women living alone, companionship in what she calls her "community of friends," two men and two women whom she meets frequently for dinner. There is something symbolic for her about sharing the experience of breaking bread. . . . Other women have structural ways of dealing with loneliness. Planning activities is a favorite way to make oneself busy. Classes (a woman of 30 learned to swim), projects, getting in-

volved in cultural groups, little theater, food co-ops—all are good ways to meet friends. But the search for time-fillers can become compulsive.

The freedom to make one's own decisions is the thing that every woman mentioned as the best part of living alone. Another word that was said again and again: privacy. To come home to peace, to wake up in the morning and not have to relate to anyone, to decide alone what to do with one's evening, day, life. Responsibility for their existence is not a burden to the woman interviewed; it is a blessing. It means freedom—freedom to exercise or belly dance or paint (badly), to watch TV or read or do nothing at all. Living alone makes a woman aware of her options. . . . Surprisingly, though, only a few of the women had pets or plants.[2]

My personal reaction to these articles is that single persons who extol the benefits of the single life while deprecating married life fall into one or more of the following categories:

1. Those people who, by nature, are what we might call very private people.
2. Schizoid personalities, who are alone whether or not anyone else is around.
3. Homosexuals, who do not wish to form a more or less permanent liason—which I might call a marriage—or who are between relationships.
4. Those who for some reason feel the need to rationalize their singleness. They fall into the "sweet lemon" category.
5. Those who have married and, now divorced, feel better if they disparage marriage. They are the "sour grapes" singles.
6. Those committed to some religious ideal, or self-concept, which precludes marriage.
7. Singles who are exploiting the single state for all it is worth. They cherish their freedom to play honeybee.
8. Those whom nobody seems to want as their very own,

or whose standards for a prospective mate are not warranted by their own market value.

9. Those who have never loved, or who just are not ready yet to love some one person over a long period of time.

10. Those for whom romantic love is just not very important. For them, marriage would be an unwelcome hindrance to the fulfillment of their life plans.

11. The severely romantic; psychosexually immature or ambivalent; psychotic; those who cannot leave home and parents; people who "learned" early in life not to trust, or love, or otherwise make themselves vulnerable; the emotionally insulated; people whose age or physical and/or intellectual disabilities make marriage difficult or impossible.

Maybe, just maybe, some people are not meant to marry. It is hard to know what to think or how to react to a single person when he or she makes such statements as the following ones made by a single woman whose book extolled the benefits and joys of single life: "There is a beautiful security. God can replace the emptyness in any lonely life with purposeful activity."[3] Her skepticism about the validity and lastingness of life is suggested by her conviction that "Jesus Christ is the only escape from loneliness that has duration."[4] Devotion to Christ as justification, or rationalization, for the desirability of the single life finds its biblical source in St. Paul's utterance that: "He that is unmarried careth for the things that belong to the Lord, that he may please the Lord."[5] At one public lecture, a male singles group leader explained that St. Paul "is speaking very positively here. He elevates that state of singleness to the point where a person can give his undivided attention to the Lord, can be totally set aside to please him, with no conflicts of interest. Because, let's face it, marriage entails responsibility, higher responsibilities, more dealing with the world, and more financial complications. Please don't misunderstand me; he is speaking positively and is encouraging the single person to realize the blessings and advantages of his singleness."[6]

Although no one can find fault with a person's dedication of his or her life to service in the work of the Lord, or to emulating the life of Christ, it is, however, important to differentiate, whenever possible, between dedication and rationalization. It is my impression that, unlike some few people who have freely chosen singleness as a way of life, most single persons who say that they *have* the best of it are really *making* the best of it.

The millions of Americans who are, right now, single could be analyzed and categorized into probably dozens of subgroups. For the purpose of studying the relationships between the church and single persons, I shall divide single persons into two basic groups: 1) Those who intend to remain single (Permanent Singles) and 2) Those who hope not to remain single (Temporary Singles).

Although these two groups differ from one another in many ways, they are much more alike than they are unlike. What they have in common is what brings them together, and perhaps to church. Some people have never really been single; they went from parents to spouse to the grave. Others have, emotionally at least, been single; alone all their lives. A larger number of us, including we who left our parents and did not marry for years, we who have been divorced one or more times, and the widows and widowers among us, we know what being single is like; it hurts. As I outlined in "First Mother, Now You,"[7] I believe that people marry because they do not want to be alone any longer and, ironically, their fear of being abandoned causes them to remain uncommitted to a marriage that they are afraid to terminate.

People are not usually fully honest when they are asked how they like being single. On the positive side, they proclaim such benefits as "privacy, freedom, lack of responsibility, exclusive use of their earnings; sequential love relationships; geographical, employment, and residential mobility; scheduling of their time and activities; total dedication to their careers, establishing of their own moods, and at least fifty more rewarding reasons for remaining single." It is said that we tend to forget or repress pain. That we really do not forget is attested by the extraordinary lengths we go to in an effort not to reexperience some painful period or incident from the past. If we are to understand and be of some service to single persons, we must learn, or remember, what it can be like to be alone. A few years ago, after fifteen years of marriage, I found myself divorced. For a while, because I was then writing a book on marriage and divorce, I kept a diary. I would like you to read some excerpts from one of the bad days:

"Why did I wake up so early? I think I'll just have some coffee—I'm glad it's Monday; lots to do at work today. . . . I wonder if anybody's going to lunch now? I'll ask Ed, he's a very understanding guy. . . . Hmmmm, everybody's gone home; guess I'm the only one who's really interested in doing a full day's work! Sure is quiet around here. I might as well go to dinner. Where? Don't want to go to Reuben's, it's so dark in there you can't read. I wonder what my kids are doing right now—probably sitting down to dinner, chattering and fussing and giggling. I used to yell at them to be quiet—never thought I'd miss the noise. Maybe I'll stop at the hamburger place—no, I feel unreal and invisible there. I could go where I went last night—the waitress there is friendly, and the hostess remembers me. What a baby; so lonesome, I'm grateful if someone remembers that they've seen me before. Oh hell, I'll go home. Baretta is on tonight. . . . It just occurred to me, I can't remember what the hell I put in the oven! I've got the TV on, the stereo playing in the bedroom, a magazine in my hand—this is silly. I'm not a basket case! There, I've turned off the radio and TV and I'm not reading. Just eating. Nothing wrong with a sandwich and soup; it's not worth it to cook for just one person . . . the phone's ringing. Maybe it's . . . . 'Hello. Who? No, you have the wrong number. That's all right! Damn! I think I'll call that girl I met last week. Nah, I don't really want to see *her*. God but that bar I met her at was depressing! Blaring music—they said it was music—those blinking colored lights and the people! Girls sitting around pretending to be having a good time talking to each other and smiling; guys circling around looking for a likely victim—like vultures. You ask a girl to dance, try to charm the pants off her—literally—take her back to the table and wait for the verdict: Does she ask you to sit down or does she thank you and turn to pick up her conversation with her girl friends? I felt degraded. I'm not *that* hard up! Am I? . . . I feel very sad, but not like crying—more like screaming. . . . I can't concentrate on this book; I may as well go to bed—but I'm not sleepy. My stomach and face feel hot like they do when I'm scared—or anxious. I guess that's it: I'm anxious. Good thing I don't drink much, otherwise I'd become an alcoholic. . . . I'm still not used to being in bed alone; I don't like it. . . . I wonder if God gets tired of my asking for the same thing every night—for some-one to love me. I wish I hadn't had to change churches, but I just couldn't take seeing my family and, even when I went to a different service, I felt so—conspicious and awkward. It wasn't any better when I went to the other place; everybody was polite and friendly—you'd have thought I was a new cus-tomer. As far as I could tell, there weren't any other single people there—but then how can you tell who is single? Maybe if I yelled, 'Is anybody there? Is anyone here alone?' someone would answer. . . . Guess I'll go to bed; that's one way of being unconcious."

My single days were not all unhappy, nor was being single all bad. But I know that what I experienced was not unusual. An interesting verification and measurement of the effects of being placed in the position of being alone is offered by psychiatrist Thomas H. Holmes of the University School of Medicine. He has developed a scale to measure the relative stress induced by various changes in a person's life. Some il-lustrative incidents and the price they exact are:

Minor violation of the law	11 points
Change in church activities	19 points
Death of a close friend	37 points
Marriage	50 points
Death of a close family member	63 points
Marital Separation	65 points
Divorce	73 points
Death of Spouse	100 points

Any counselor will verify that the clients who manifest the greatest anxiety, depression, and disinclination to live are those who feel abandoned and alone. While it is true that most recover and their psychic wounds heal, often the scar tissue becomes adhesions, which restrict their capacity for loving. It is my premise that all but a few single persons want more intimacy and continuity of interpersonal relationships. So that we can proceed to an examination of what the church can and should offer single persons, we need to look briefly at the kind of world in which this would take place.

3

Alone Together

The young man was like most any other you might find lean-
ing against a bar in a pose intended to convey casualness,
confidence, and coolness. One hand held a cocktail, which he
didn't really want, while his left hand tapped rhythmi-
cally—suggesting a self-containment that he did not feel. He
remembered me, and he was relieved to have someone to talk
to.

"Why do I come here?" he said. "I don't know. I never
thought about it. The music, I guess, and the dancing. I really
dig dancing and, of course, the chicks that come here—
they're a lotta fun, and no obligation even when you spend
the night at their place. This is really a swinging place.
Everything you'd want—"

His speech ceased and he nervously gulped at his drink.
"You don't believe me, do you? Well, that's OK. I don't
believe me either. I don't know what I'm doing here, but it's
better than being alone. I mean, that's the way it is
nowadays: Do your thing and look out for yourself. Besides,
what's the alternative? Marriage? Responsibility? Looking to
the future? What future? What's the point of it all anyhow?"

If we study this man's explanation as to why he frequented
discotheques and bars, we see that he is seeking *social inter-*

action (he doesn't want to be alone) and *activity* (dancing is preferable to being alone). He appears to have resigned himself to a lack of both *meaning* in his life (what's the point of it all?) and *intimacy* (no obligation; avoidance of marriage and responsibility).

She was a pretty woman, thirty-two, a widow with three children, assistant manager of the bookstore at the college where I teach. We were having coffee, and I told her that she looked kind of down today.

"Down?" she asked. "Maybe so. I've been this way for so long that it seems natural to me. I guess I'm tired. Tired of giving, tired of being busy, tired of being tired."

"Do you still go to the church you were telling me about last summer?" I asked.

"No, not any more. I like the minister; his sermons are really worth listening to. But I felt invisible there—like no one knew what to do with me. It just wasn't a—" Here she hesitated.

"You mean it wasn't very personal?" I questioned.

"Yes, but it was more than that. There didn't seem to be any way for me to get involved or to be anything other than a passive participant. I didn't feel that the church was having any impact on me—either emotionally or intellectually. I want to better myself, but I need help to do that. I don't like to admit it, but I was hoping to meet some single men there, too, or at least make some warm friends. I don't know. Maybe I expected too much. Maybe I have to accept the fact that a church can't be a second family for me."

My friend, the former church member, had specified several things, which she had sought in vain in her church: inspiration, recognition, warmth or affection, the opportunity to make a contribution, self-improvement, new friends—including maybe a boyfriend, and, most important of all, a substitute family. She no longer believes that she can find what she needs in a church environment.

Single persons, whether they are young or old, divorced, widowed, or never married, whether you meet them at singles clubs, bars, Parents without Partners, senior citizens centers, the YMCA or at church, have the same basic needs and goals as do married people. They differ only in that they are in the position of trying to meet their needs *alone.* If one wishes to evaluate the success with which an institution is fulfilling its goals, it is necessary to have some criteria or standards of measurement. Below is a list of what I believe SPs are looking for, and which churches, with variable success, attempt to provide:

1. Love
2. Meaning
3. Support
4. Social interaction
5. Self-growth
6. Activity
7. Intimacy
8. Spiritual fulfillment

Being a clinical psychologist, I tend to see everything in a psychological frame of reference. So, let's look at what some clergymen see SPs as needing. A Baptist minister in Texas suggests that the church can best serve SPs by:

1. Providing channels for healthy singles relationships.
2. Reconsidering its attitude toward divorced persons.
3. Assisting the formerly married to find friendships that will offer spiritual nurture.
4. Recognizing various levels of personal and spiritual development among singles.
5. Recognizing singles participation in the church and commending them.
6. Recognizing the importance of "the family of God in the life of singles."[1]

The above list is representative of what might be termed a "church frame of reference." Certainly the above six recommendations cannot be criticized for their placing a heavy emphasis upon accepting SPs as being worthy of the church's acceptance and concern. It is likely, however, that many SPs would feel that such a list conveys a patronizing attitude toward the unmarried. Nor did the writer display much awareness of the SPs needs apart from the church. In short, SPs do not feel complimented or uplifted by a church's admission that "We're OK, you're OK."

A more psychologically sophisticated conception of SPs needs is offered by Rev. Jim Smoke of Garden Grove Community Church in California:

> Singles have four basic needs. The first is a *relational* need. The business world has verified this by grouping singles together for different activities. Most singles are interested in building relationships with other singles. A second need is for *social interaction.* Any creative singles program, whether secular or spiritual, will offer a variety of social activities. A third need is often a *spiritual* one. We have found that many singles who have experienced divorce tend to drift back to the church seeking spiritual answers and growth. People reaching for spiritual direction relate more easily to a warm, positive, Christian presentation than to a cold, condemning, judgemental one. A fourth need is *education.* We attempt to meet this need by offering specialized courses to singles such as "The Single Person's Indentity," in which we explore the spiritual basis for building right relationships. Another titled "How to Handle Divorce" deals with such topics as The Emotional Side of Divorce, Raising Children in a Single Parent Home, Singles and Sexuality, the Ex-Spouse, Remarriage, Beginning Again, What the Scriptures Teach about Divorce, and many other helpful things. Resource people from our church and professional counselors throughout the area are used to host special seminars and lectures that deal directly with the needs of singles in all areas.[2]

Mr. Smoke's four points are a great improvement on the programs and philosophy relating to SPs that characterized churches until very recently. The program that he briefly discusses is professional, comprehensive, attractive, and successful. But, as I shall discuss further on, a program can be popular without being personal.

Churches all over America are trying to expand and improve their service to SPs. They are trying very hard, but being institutions—often very large ones—they fall prey to the problems and temptations of all institutions. In his book, *Your Fear of Love*, psychologist Marshall Hodge wrote that

> Despite lip service to the primacy of love in human relationships, the church, by and large, tends in practice to see moral value primarily in terms of external behavior rather than in terms of experience and love.[3]

He adds that

> Religious groups, like people in general, have not understood their fear of intimacy. Without realizing it, they have encouraged emotional distance between people rather than the experience of love they professed to promote. For example, churces often substitute apparent expressions of love for the experience of intimacy.[4]

Dr. Hodge is pointing out some distinctions which *must be* recognized by any church that hopes to bring spiritual comfort to its members—particularly those members whose inner psyches are battered and raw from the trauma of rejection or loneliness. In evaluating these church programs, including those directed at SPs, it is imperative that we distinguish between proximity and intimacy, action and interaction, and *expressions* of love instead of *feelings* of love.

The fact that large numbers of SPs are in company with each other and enjoying it does not constitute evidence that they are really in close relationship to each other. Roman Catholic Stephen Clark defines a Christian community as

> an environment of Christians which can provide for the basic needs of its members to live the Christian life. . . .

> There must be interaction between the people in the social grouping that is personal, that is, relationship-oriented and not just task-oriented.[5]

His statement serves as a warning to us that we not define a successful group or program as merely being a hive of people buzzing busily around performing tasks and taking care not to get too close to each other. Many church singles programs are like that.

The following is a definition of *community*, which I believe any truly worthwhile singles group must approximate; it is offered by the Rev. Michael Scanlon.

> A true community church is one where the giving of each member is to the point where each accepts responsibility for the other and shares his very self. The teaching of the New Testament is that there is special power available to those who come together in the name of Jesus. The church is meant to have the note of togetherness, fellowship, or "Koinonia." Koinonia is essential to the church and those ministries that do not flow from togetherness in the Lord will necessarily lack power.[6]

I am convinced that no church can hope to meet all or most of the eight basic needs, which I listed earlier, unless that church—or at least its singles group—is a *community* embodying fellowship, intimacy, spirituality, and love. When a church begins to measure its success primarily in terms of number, economics, and status, it has begun to die as a church. The same principle applies to persons as well as to institutions.

> Somewhere in his development he began to measure the value of his total personality or character by the *number* of his *achievements*. Moreover, these achievements invariably must be those he believes capture the respect and admiration of his peers and superiors. He does not,

however, care whether the achievements gain him the love or affection of his fellow men, although he does not particularly care to be disliked.[7]

The foregoing is a description of the kind of personal value system that can lead to death, first of the spirit and then of the body. Neither an SP or a singles group can survive in spirit unless they are motivated by the intent to give and receive *love*. In the list of eight basic needs of the SP which I listed, love is the most important. Without love (*agape* or *filios*) as the starting point, and the end point, the other seven needs can only be temporarily quaffed—never fulfilled.

Nowadays, in the language of the young, love and feelings are "in." No more being satisfied with order, predictability, control, logic, or intellectual truth. We are now being encouraged to seek and demand emotional stimulation and satisfaction. The same refocus has taken place in the field of psychotherapy. Insight and understanding are not enough; they are not even necessary. Among many "modern" psychotherapists, what counts is what you feel—and what you *must* feel is to feel good. Even feeling bad is said to feel good if you are sticking with and owning your own feelings, letting it all hang out, and avoiding "bad trips." No area of human activity has escaped being affected by the "gospel" of feeling and sensation. Being civilized, our tendency is to rationalize our experience of our feelings by coupling them with some philosophical or theological value system. It is said that we value that for which we pay a high price. Let's see if that maxim can help us to better understand what is happening in American churches—particularly with reference to church attendance in general and singles programs in particular.

Anyone who has attended a middle class "successful" church has found that what happens is nice, respectable, and predictable, which is how most people hope their lives will be. People whose life goals were designed to afford relief from the emotional stresses of wars, riots, financial problems, religious uncertainty, nuclear bombs, a shakiness, in fact, of every aspect of their existence—these people understandably appreciate a calm, orderly, "sensible" way of life. Their children, however, are not appreciative, or even accepting, of what they feel to be "the older generation's" bland, intellectualized life-style; their use and misuse of existential philosophy and humanistic psychology leads to an impatient rejection of what they consider to be "the old way of life." They are expressing subjective assurance that "the means of ultimate transformation is available *here* and that the transformation is taking place in them *now*."[8] Young people, most of them single, by the millions are joining religious groups which promise interpersonal involvement and emotional experiences—quickly.

> In a time of uncertainty and dissatisfaction with the cold, impersonal, formal worship of the "mainline denominations," participating in an ecstatic worship is refreshing. For someone weary of academic discussion or theological questions, or impatient with the lukewarm committment of many members of established churches, speaking in tongues satisfies a hunger for an authoritative, immediate, personal, and powerful religious experience.[9]

Religious experiences that are emotionally charged, as is true in glossalalia, witnessing, ocean baptism, altar calls, spiritual healing, spontaneous public praying, and Konionia groups, are attracting millions of preforties people whose personal lives otherwise embody little in the way of intensive feelings. Single persons, especially, are hungry for some increments of feeling, intimacy, and spirituality in their otherwise mundane, impersonal existences. Feeling low, they thirst for a high; living in the physical, they turn to the metaphysical; inwardly alone, they cling together. And many of them are attending churches where they can pray together and play together. Whether they will stay together is another question.

A warning as to what can happen to those whose religious or social involvements are motivated by a search for a "fix" and a "high" was voiced by psychologist Abraham Maslow:

If the sole good in life becomes the peak-experience, and if all means to this end become good, and if more peak-experiences are better than fewer, then one can *force* the issue, push actively, strive and hurt and fight for them. So they have often moved over into magic, into the secret and esoteric, the occult, the dramatic and effortful, the dangerous and the cultish. Healthy openness to the mysterious, the realistically humble recognition that we don't know much, the modest and graceful acceptance of gratuitous grace and just plain good luck—all these can shade over into the anti-rational, the anti-emperical, the anti-scientific, the anti-verbal, the anti-conceptual.[10]

Maslow is right: to a point, healthy individuals and institutions are characterized by a balance between the cognitive and the affective. Thinking and feeling complement each other. When too much emphasis is placed upon one end of the continuum, the other end shrivels. In the excitement and thrill of a personal breakthrough into a new insight or emotion, there is great danger of becoming one-dimensional. One of the programs, or techniques, or put-ons of the seventies is something called EST. In an evangelical book on EST, a writer inadvertently illustrates how lonely, bewildered people can engage in a self-development program which, I believe, leaves them as disproportionally developed as is the weight lifter with a massive torso teetering on skinny legs. Study the two quotations that follow, and then visualize the EST graduate's emotional experience as compared with his intellectual development. The author gives his own opinion in the first statement:

What EST does have in common with Western religion is the sense of service, of mission, and of course its definition of a way of being and experiencing.

This experience of belonging—in a special place, with a particular group of people—was once provided by one's church. Today an EST graduate might put in long hours of painstaking work and have such an experience—a sense of belonging, of serving. I've seen a similar kind of fervor among volunteer workers in a political campaign. The difference between the EST and the political volunteer is that EST-ers experience satisfaction in their lives and activists can merely *hope* that their efforts will change their lives.[11]

This next statement was made by EST designer Werner Erhardt:

A belief system is a myth, created by knowledge or data without experience. If you experience something, it is real for you, and if you communicate it to somebody, it is real for them. If they now tell it to somebody else, it's a lie—belief without the componant of experience.[12]

In spite of such inane profundities, EST is flourishing. Its graduates are true evangelists, giving testimony that they have found meaning, community, and freedom—all in sixty hours. It is easy for me, as a professional psychologist, to decry the lack of a scientific theoretical and experimental basis for the EST program. I can show that it is a potpourri of philosophical and psychological systems, a skillfully marketed caricature of a personal growth program. And yet, when I talk with an EST graduate, I cannot shut out his enthusiastic conviction that he has found the truth and has undergone a transformation of mind and spirit. If I listen carefully, a chilling realization forms: He is a convert to a new gospel propounded by a marketing messiah. He promises a life of freedom and meaning to all who undergo prescribed rites of confession, catharsis, and commitment to the cause. He will not join a singles group—for he is a member of the "EST-ers." He may very well find a church superfluous, for he has found something to live by and for.

EST is not unlike many of the new therapies offered by psychologists, psychiatrists, social workers, counselors, facilitators, masseurs, doctors, enablers, mental health workers, paraprofessionals, and myriad other professional and amateur helpers. Each has been trained in one or more systems of

psychotherapy. They promise their patients, clients, coun-
selees, students, and other novices that association with them
and their group will mean an end to pain, loneliness, and the
anxiety of being human. All have some success; some have
great success. They appear, flourish, and disappear—leaving
behind disenchanted and diminished human beings. What is
their secret? What do they give for what they take? What can
we learn from them that will help us to better prepare our
churches for their mission of ministering to those in need of
physical, intellectual, emotional, and spiritual sustenance?

It is easy to ascertain what people want; it is more difficult
to determine what they need and how to give it to them. I
have studied church singles programs whose membership
was in the hundreds. I have spent evenings in other churches
whose singles group numbered ten or fifteen. I can assure you
that often there is no correlation between statistical success
and church mission. This is true in spite of every church
leader's dream of extending the Gospel to as many people as
possible. What I shall attempt to do, then, is to identify those
characteristics of various church singles groups that will
assist us in offering the greatest good to the greatest number
of single persons.

"Relevancy" is one of today's standards against which we
measure the "viability" (another of today's wonder words) of
an idea or program. "Is it relevant?" was a question we
began asking when we found ourselves possessing the knowledge and freedom to no longer function in a passive relationship to authorities offering past solutions to present problems. Humanitarians and activists demanded "bread, not
words." Predictably, institutions overreacted: people-
teachers became people-pleasers. Nowhere was this more
true than among churches. This emphasis on "relevancy"
and "giving 'em what they want" radiated from headquar-
ters to pulpit to groups within the church—particularly to
singles groups. Some of our more statistically successful
singles programs are as empty of meaning and spiritual
values as are most of the modern systems of psychotherapy.

Since I believe that what has happened recently in the profession of counseling is analogous to current trends in the church-related groups, I would like to briefly trace how the philosophy and practice of counseling has changed, in two particular ways, for the worse.

Regardless of the "denominational" appellation: transactional analysis, Gestalt, Rolfing, rational-emotive, bioenergetics, or encounter, counseling clients nowadays believe that they are taught that:

> 1. Everything is relative. Right and wrong can be determined within the specific situation. You have a right to do your own thing. You are responsible for your own actions, but you cannot be responsible for others. Life is, essentially, meaningless; so enjoy yourself ("You only go around once"). The past is dead, the future is unreal, and the present is unsure. Beliefs are myths. Love is transient. God is dead, or he has been identified as the Wizard of Oz.
>
> 2. Feelings are what count—as long as they are gut level. Values and standards are rationalizations for emotional inhibition. Thinking is a cop out, a head trip, a denial of the fact that we are, essentially, beings of sensation and emotion. Your emotions are more trustworthy than are your thoughts ("If it feels good, do it"). Love is possessive ("You can't own anyone"). Ultimate personal truths are to be found in the body. As long as you don't hurt anyone else, it's OK—hurting yourself means to deny yourself ("Eat, drink, and be merry, for tomorrow you may be alive"). Life is a drag, so "turn on" however you can.

Speaking as a completely biased person, I consider the philosophical stance outlined above to be stupid, amoral, hedonistic, primitive, and destructive. Psychotherapists did not give birth to the new morality, but we have helped to deliver and nourish it. Should you think my concern is exaggerated, look in the movie section of your Sunday newspaper; try to find a movie that you would consider to be entertaining *and* educational or edifying for yourself, much less for your children. After eliminating those that deal with mass murder, catastrophes such as earthquakes, tidal waves, blazing infernos, outer space monsters, witchcraft, rape, psychosis, sexual orgies, infidelity, homosexuality, destruction of the earth, and exposing of the basically evil nature of man, I found myself faced with three movies I had already seen. Thank God for Mel Brooks and Walt Disney!

Why are so many people drawn to vicarious participation in every conceivable kind of horror? One explanation is that we can thereby externalize the horrors lurking in the recesses of our own minds: our personal demons are recognized and vanquished in their disguise as the misfortune and tragedies of others. Too, and this is most relevant to our inquiry as to how we can draw people close so that we may be of service to them, people are searching for something—anything—that will make them *feel*. The churches, or at least some of them, have been caught up in the demand being made by many people, especially young people, for experiences that are emotionally provocative. Single persons constitute a large proportion of those who have joined what has been termed the charismatic movement. They are intolerant of the old way. They are demanding that their religion be exciting, personal, decisive, and demanding; their fervor is in opposition to recent religious trends.

> We have apologetically eliminated all sanctions of external discipline, thereby giving notice to all the world that a half-hearted response to the Gospel is better than none, and created the monstrosity of a church dominated by the mildly attracted.[13]

Sounds reasonable, doesn't it? Even hopeful. But, as we shall see, many church singles groups are designed for those people who, in a religious sense, are mildly attracted.

Other single persons want more than is offered them by those churches that are satisfied with a traditional, and bland, relationship with and between its members.

The established church seems to be traditional in its ways, impersonal in its approach to outsiders and even towards its own members. It appears to be like a machine that is interested more in keeping moving and keeping its gears oiled than in developing spiritual insight and experience in the lives of its members. Especially young people want to be thought of not as parts of a machine, but as unique persons. They thus become disgruntled with the church and its practices. At this point they seek out more personal organizations, leaders who relate to them more individually and personally, who treat them as valid persons, and who communicate personalness to them. . . . Too often in the impersonal church the individual feels unwanted, rejected, and alienated.[14]

So, while some people seek a mild religious affiliation, others require a more intense experience. With a little shopping around and sampling, one can find whatever style of church experience one wishes. And that is what this book is concerned with: What can, and should, the church do to attract single persons—and what should it do with them after they get there?

4

A Meeting Place

Just as there seem to be an infinite diversity of personality types that, when studied, can be sorted into a few basic types, so is there an apparently wide range of church singles groups that can be classified with reference to their personalness and their relationship to the church. It is important that we realize that many ministers are not enthusiastic about the usefulness, or even the appropriateness, of devoting church resources to the fostering of singles activities. A forty-two-year-old Episcopal rector of a church of 250 communicants explained why he has chosen not to encourage a singles program in his own church:

> "I don't have time for that sort of thing, and if I did have some extra time, I wouldn't spend it playing shepherd to lonely unmarrieds. There are a lot more important things to be done, such as social action and bringing the Gospel into the arenas of business, politics and education. Sure, single people have needs peculiar to their unmarried status—particularly divorced people—but we can't set up a special program for every subpopulation in the church. We try to involve everybody in church functions; our goal is to have everyone—married, single, old, young—*integrated*, not just affiliated, into every

phase of the church's activites. If a single person wants a place to worship and to interact with other Christians, he or she would be comfortable in our church. But if all they want is a place for meeting someone to date, I'd rather they went somewhere else."

The points of concern expressed by this minister, and many others whom we interviewed, were:

1. Single people are especially interested in socializing.
2. The church is not a social center.
3. Church singles work has a low priority.

Whether or not a church chooses to concern itself with "the singles problem" is, basically, a philosophical decision. As we shall see, that philosophy can be inferred from the kind of singles program that a particular church offers.

Sooner or later, someone was bound to ask: "Why not have a special church, a church just for single persons?" One man who asked the question, and then proceeded to formulate an answer, is the Reverend Richard Chen. He first came to national attention through a story that appeared in *Newsweek* June 12, 1972. The article relates that the Church of 100 Communicants, including some divorcees who have remarried,

aims to serve adults with "spiritual and social needs that are different from those of people who are married. Single people are lonely in a couple-oriented society. Traditionally, churches don't know what to do with singles. . . . The person who needs help comes away feeling like an outcast and often leave the church altogether." To supplement the Sunday services, Chen conducts a monthly seminar in which the congregation discusses problems common to singles and has organized a pastoral counseling team whose ten members have been trained "to listen, to have empathy and to offer friendship." Inevitably, some prospective

members regard the church as some sort of sanctified dating bureau. "A lot of people come once or twice," admits Chen. "Often, if they don't find Mr. or Mrs. Right, they don't come back. But others come here because they want companionship and have spiritual needs.
Churches have been losing ground for years because they haven't kept up with social needs. People who are alone want a church they can feel comfortable in. Ours is a regular church, just like any other—except that our members often arrive alone.[1]

Four years later, we interviewed Mr. Chen in hopes of learning how his church had fared. He sadly informed us that his church for singles had survived for but three years. In his opinion, singles are a transient group without stability; that their primary goal is to meet someone, and that they were drawn to his church for that reason. He explained that although he had a core of workers, many of those got married—some to each other. As he lost his core of single workers, his church inevitably declined. Although Rev. Chen did not attempt to make excuses, it appears that his church attracted singles who were in a state of flux, not stable financially or committed; their committment to the singles church was tenuous. Apparently having singleness in common was not enough to bind them for long to this particular church.

Other institutions whose membership consists solely of single persons face the same self-defeating characteristic: The factor that qualifies one for membership is one that one usually changes—which will disqualify one for membership. Certainly groups such as Parents without Partners, Boy Scouts, and church youth groups all have learned that they cannot survive without an administrative staff, which will remain while members come and go. In general, a church singles group that is intended to flourish, or even survive, must assure that the core of its leadership—even if it is from outside the group—must consist of people who, regardless of their marital state, are committed to continuing membership in that particular church. Continuity of internal membership is for some church singles groups, assured by virtue of the membership of single persons who have no intention or desire to give up their single status. The advantages and disadvantages of this kind of leadership merit our attention in a later chapter.

At one extreme is the church that is devoted exclusively to single persons; at the other extreme are the churches that have evinced no discernable interest in singles' problems. One step up from the latter attitude are the churches that sponsor, or host, singles groups. A student of mine recently attended a singles-only weekend sponsored by one of the less theistically oriented denominations. She spoke enthusiastically of cookouts, nude swimming, campfire sings, coed room accomodations, arts and crafts demonstrations, yoga and aikido lessons, lectures on ecology, and, best of all, an optional "Tom Jones banquet in the forest—finger lickin' good." I did not believe her. Two weeks later, she mailed me a flyer advertising that church's next singles sortie to the moutains. After reading such items as "Our heated pool will be available—suits optional—exercise a little caution here for the sun can burn you more readily at high altitudes. . . . Things to share: a bottle of wine or your favorite poetry, your musical instrument—whatever turns you on! . . . Outdoor art workshop with live model!" Now I believe her.

For those whose idea of a religious experience requires only such ingredients as companionship, the outdoors, play, and freedom from social restraints, the "Tom Jones Special" will be a satisfying meal. Those single persons whose spiritual and psychological tastes are of a higher order would leave such a session with their hunger unsatisfied; they might even feel sick at their stomachs.

A more conventional form of church sponsorship of singles activities is that described in a *New York Times* article, which was referred to earlier. It describes a "Single Again" group for the formerly married, which is sponsored by the Universalist Church on Central Park West at 76th Street:

> From 150 to 200 name-tagged people pay $3 to socialize at the church, enjoying refreshments for an hour or so,

split into seven or eight "rap" groups, and later renew the socializing process. The "rap" group is a key element in this type of singles social. It brings people together in small groups, with a leader, to discuss a topic. The topic often has to do with relationships with the opposite sex.[2]

The article states that approximately 60 percent of the people at Single Again show up every Wednesday. One of the participants believed that "although it might not be group therapy, it gets pretty personal. But a lot of them are playing a game," he said. "It's not like group therapy, where the masks really drop."

A second singles group described in the same *Times* story was one called "Lib Woman—Lib Men," which meets at the First Unitarian Church in Brooklyn Heights!

In the church basement there are card tables covered with red-checked tablecloths and a stereo set plays, but not too raucously.

There were not only discussion groups to choose from on a recent Friday, but games as well: charades and a game called First Impression, which quickly cured the shyness and self-consciousness of several newcomers. "It was a gasser," said one participant. "A real fun blast."

At the Brotherhood Synagogue on Gramercy Park, where the ties between the synagogue and the singles groups appear to be close, singles in the 25 to 40 age group discussed vacation possibilities on a recent Monday night.

"We're avoiding the formality of a very structured rap, because people who are single over a certain age are probably single because they don't like structure," said Ernest Glogover, president of the steering committee.[3]

Not at all relieved to have been handed the answer to why people over a certain age are single, I continued on to the last of the singles programs mentioned in this *New York Times* article. The following is a short narrative of one meeting of the City Singles of Marble Collegiate Church:

> After an ample dinner of chicken, peas, baked potatoes and chocolate cream pie, for which they paid $3.50, 100 people from 35 to 50 listened to a lecture on assertiveness, and later (after coffee, tea and cookies) found partners and danced to big band music from a record player.
>
> "I come here not to meet anybody, but because I belong—there is warmth and love and concern here," said Estelle Randolph, program chairman. "I'm single and I love it. I'll never get married again. I love my freedom. I want to belong to myself.
>
> A man nodded quizically. Before spinning off with his partner in a waltz, he said, "Well, I'm still looking. I haven't ruled it out. If the right girl comes along. . . . But in the meantime, you have to make the best of it."[4]

The church singles groups we have been looking at are very similar in design, philosophy, and goals to all these groups that I have termed "church-sponsored." The only criteria that a group need meet in order to be included in this classification are that the church has lent its name and its premises as a meeting place. Some churches require that the group's leaders be members of that church, while most such groups do not require that any of its singles group participants belong to that, or any other, church. In the church-sponsored singles group (CSSG), there is little if any evidence that religious concepts or practices influence the group's functioning. This is not to say that CSSG meetings are indistinguishable from singles gatherings in bars and discotheques. Their meetings, if not spiritual, at least are decorous. The CSSG's meetings are primarily social in nature. In fact, they seem to have no other purpose for meeting.

CSSG socializing follows the pattern of social dating behavior: introductions, chatting, refreshments, chatting, a touch of serious talk, dancing, chatting, and promises to meet again. The membership appears to consist of a core of regulars, augmented by a large number of occasional attenders, and a high percentage of first-timers who do not return. Nearly every person to whom I spoke who indicated that his first time at a CSSG meeting would be his last explained his decision the same way: "This just isn't my kind of thing." Further questioning often brought the explanation that "these people here look like losers to me." Such a reaction may reflect the fact that single persons are either divorced or have not yet married, or it may reveal that the speaker is one of those "body shoppers" who are the bane of all singles groups, or it may be that person's way of rationalizing why he isn't enjoying himself.

Putting aside for a moment the question of the ultimate value of CSSG organizations, let's see what some CSSG participants like about their association with the program. At two different churches I encountered people who had been students of mine. One, a thirty-six-year-old divorcée who looked younger than her years, was very frank in her replies.

I asked her, "what do you get out of coming here?"

"Because I'm lonely, and I was losing my self-respect by going to bars and getting picked up by—or picking up—men whom I would never see again. I was even losing my women friends—some of them disapproved of my activities, and the others were competitors in the 'garage sale' atmosphere of the singles bars."

"What is it like for you here at the _____ Singles group?"

"Well," she replied, "its not very personal—people come and go; and the regulars, especially the leaders, are a real ingroup—you know, they seem more interested in expanding membership than in getting close to the newcomers. But even so, I've met some really nice people here, people I can socialize with during the week."

"Anything you'd like to change about the way the organization is run?" I asked.

"Uh, I hadn't put it into words before, but I wish there were some emphasis on religion, or at least more of a feeling that we really are connected with this church—or to some church. But don't get me wrong, I'm grateful to have a place like this to come to."

The twenty-seven-year-old man to whom I talked had never married. He was pursuing a graduate degree in business. Slight of build, articulate and assertive, he had been introduced to the _____ church singles group by a friend, who had assured him that there were "a lot of sharp chicks and not much competition" there. It would have been naïve of me to ask why he attended this CSSG's functions. Other than the fact that he could harvest the weekly crop of new female participants, he graced the meetings because, "they don't push all that religious stuff at you. Hell, if that's what I wanted, I'd go to regular church services."

My impression of the CSSG officers and leaders whom I met is that their investment of time and talent yields a high dividend for them. Although they maintain a necessary liason with the sponsoring church, their primary identification is with each other. There is no question but that the opportunities for companionship, self-growth, a feeling of belonging, and a sense of usefulness rewarded them for their contributions to the group. One cannot help but wonder how they are affected by the fact that should they marry, and since they usually have no particular involvement in the sponsoring church's general activities, they must relinquish their affiliation with a group that has meant so much to them. There is much to be said for those CSSG's which plan, and work, toward the kind of church-singles group structure (and attitude) which will allow the single person to leave the group without leaving the church.

Summary of Church-Sponsored Singles Groups

CSSG's can be initiated either by a pastor who announces that church facilities and assistance are available for use by a singles group or at the request of someone who represents a group that already exists or is being planned. All the church need do is to establish some means of nominal supervision of the group's activities. Often, the group is conceived by one or more persons within the church. These people usually expect, or want, no more church involvement than would be true if they were forming a travel club or a volleyball team. The membership that is solicited and expected can be from within or from without the church.

The format for a CSSG meeting is geared to the development of its reason for being: socializing. As far as is practical, the meeting area is made to resemble as much as possible a place where people might meet, eat, dance, and talk. In other words, nonchurchlike. Everyone's name is affixed to a stick-on tag, which is captioned "Hello." Meetings begin with the introduction of first-time guests. After one of the officers gives a brief introduction to the "rap topic" for the evening, the audience reforms into small groups, which are led by regular members who may be called discussion leaders, facilitators, or ennablers. Sometimes the evening's discussion topic is introduced by some outside expert who gives a thirty-minute talk. Other times there is a panel discussion on matters relating to the concerns of single people, such as child-raising, finances, divorce, alcoholism, love, psychological problems, and so forth. Within the small groups, subject matter and interaction are intellectual and impersonal. Personal revelation and intense emotionality are discouraged, inasmuch as the group's purpose is to foster social interaction rather than psychotherapeutic involvement. Everyone is encouraged to participate, to put aside their shyness and self-judgmentalism.

At the end of a prespecified time, the discussion groups end and they are ready to do what they came for. Music, food, drinks, games, and dancing allow the participants to shop around for someone to concentrate on or simply to have a good time being part of an informal, nonthreatening social occasion. When the general meeting is over, some participants move on together to restaurants, bars, or each other's homes. If they have made "a good connection" they may not return—they now have no need to. If they have simply had a good time, they will probably be back. A CSSG, then, exists in order to provide a nice place where people can expand their social life, meet new people, and have a good time.

Personal Opinion

Church-sponsored singles groups cost the church very little in terms of personnel, money, or time. In the sense of cost effectiveness, CSSGs are a good investment, for they yield a high dividend with little down. Among the benefits to a church of sponsoring (housing, endorsing) a singles group are:

1. Enhancement of the church's image as being concerned with people's "real" problems.
2. Publicity (which is not the same as public relations).
3. A chance to introduce religious philosophy to people who might never be exposed to it.
4. The probability that some participants will become members of the church.
5. An opportunity to experiment, and to learn, about group programs.
6. Some financial return as payment for use of church facilities.
7. Increasing the likelihood that church members who are single will remain in the church.
8. An opportunity to establish a personal identification that might motivate a single person to join one of the church's other groups when he or she marries, e.g. couple groups, children and family programs.
9. A means of developing a deeper understanding of the special problems and needs of a large number of people.
10. The opportunity of giving without expecting much in return.

Despite benefits to the church and to the CSSG participants—and the above list does not exhaust the potential pluses of CSSGs, I have some misgiving about them. Most of all, I resent the lost opportunities to bring the Gospel to life, to show that the church can live up to its promise as a center for spiritual comfort, education, and growth. Everyone is lonely, some more than others. Single people need help in finding and knowing not only each other, but also themselves; and if they freely choose to attend a singles group that is church sponsored, they should be given an opportunity to learn that loneliness and a search for meaning is more than a matter simply of making friends and having something to look forward to next week. As one clergyman has phrased it, "What religion is doing in every instance (albeit with greater or lesser effectiveness) is *explaining the meaning of life in ultimate terms.*"[5]

Although I consider it appropriate that a church should assist another group to develop and sustain a program designed to reduce emotional pain and, perhaps, to foster loving relationships between people, I do not consider it appropriate for a church to lend its name to an organization that has little if any involvement with matters religious. This does not imply that the sponsoring church should, or has any right to, attempt to take over the singles group leadership. Nor do I wish to conjure up images of evangelical double agents slinking around drumming up business for the church. No, not that; but it is possible and seemly for group programs and meetings to include some aspects of religious life, such as prayer, song, devotions such as evening prayer, panel discussions, and lectures on philosophical, psychological, and religious topics. It has been said that the best way to make a friend is to let someone do a favor for you; perhaps the best way to bring a singles group *into* the church is to encourage it to perform some service to the church.

Finally, it is important that some of the membership, especially officers and leaders, be members of the sponsoring church. This overlapping commitment is necessary if the church is to be more than a meeting place. When this kind of church-singles group relationship has been effected the church-sponsored singles group will have matured into the type of group we shall study in the next chapter: the church-related singles group.

5

The Church-Related
Singles Group

The term "Church Singles Group" does not, as we are learning, tell us very much about what the relationship is between a particular church and the singles group that is associated with it. In terms of a greater closeness, or involvement, or reciprocal interaction, from the church-sponsored singles group (CSSG), the next step is the church-related singles group (CRSG). It is the thesis of this book that the character and quality of a church's participation in its singles group determines the character and quality of that group's efforts. Some churches apparently are satisfied with providing respectability, identity, a physical site, some organizational assistance, and even a few members as its contribution to single persons *qua* singles persons. There is no specific or explicit effort made by the church leaders to have an influence on the organization or its members. In other words, the church does not attempt to bring religion into the singles group. This type of relationship was studied in the preceding chapter. There are other churches that are not satisfied with merely sponsoring: They want to be *related*.

In his book, *Why Conservative Churches Are Growing*, Dean M. Kelley analyzes the self-defeating tactics of churches that overaccomodate to secular trends:

Since the incentives held out by the liberal churches—fellowship, entertainment, knowledge (about personality and adjustment, women's liberation, home management, and so on) respectability, etc.—are offered by many other (non-religious) groups, those churches place themselves in competition for adherents with organizations which may have more compelling forms of the same attractions."[1]

Kelley proposes several emphases that might serve to halt the current decline in liberal church enrollments. It would be well for you to consider them carefully, and refer to them later as we examine two CRSGs that are, statistically at least, very successful:

1. A more contemporary liturgy, making fuller use of the arts.
2. Better and more professional counseling.
3. A revival of great preaching.
4. New methods and media of evangelism.
5. Identification with the empowerment of oppressed minorities.
6. Greater empathy with the youth culture.
7. A return to the Bible.
8. Cultivation of gifts of the Spirit: speaking in tongues, prophecy, faith healing, etc.
9. A stronger program of stewardship.
10. More time and money for religious education.[2]

Two Baptist churches that are heavily involved in ministering to singles are the First Baptist Church of Van Nuys, California, and the South Main Baptist Church of Houston, Texas. The former church offers singles programs and singles groups. In March 1976, it sponsored a three-day conference of workshops and speakers from various professions in a program devoted to assisting single persons. The Houston Church offers an innovative, and needed, program of support groups for recently divorced persons. Although the thrust is toward helping people to make it through the emotionally painful holiday period, their groups meet for at least six months.

When I inquired of a Roman Catholic priest friend as to what the Catholic Church was doing with and for single persons, he referred me to the organization set up for Catholic singles in Orange County, California. Since my fantasies of being mistaken for a young single had been shattered early in my research, I asked Ms. Arlene Roehm, the young woman who has been my research associate in this project, to spend some time with the Catholic Alumni Club. Following is a copy of this group's social calendar, and Ms. Arlene Roehm's evaluation:

August
1. General meeting at the Hyatt House
2. Home Mass
3. Softball
4. Bridge
5. Volleyball
6. Knotts' Berry Farm—Chicken Dinner, Square Dance at the Sheraton
7. Disneyland and Dinner
8. Convention alumni night at the Hotel del Coronado in San Diego
10. Softball
11. Bridge
12. Volleyball
14. Birthday party
17. Laguna Beach Pageant of the Masters
18. Bridge
19. Volleyball
20. TGIF at Charlie Brown's
22. Fourth Sunday Mass
25. Bridge; Volleyball
26. Volleyball
28. Cool-off Barbecue
29. Volleyball Pizza Party
30. Home Mass

"This is the Orange Co. branch of a national organization for Catholics who are single, over twenty-one, and have a college degree. There is a Catholic coordination committee who can direct you to the right group: Catholic divorced people, Catholic young people, Catholic etc., etc. They seem to be structured organizationally in every direction.

"This monthly meeting is primarily a business meeting. Usually 100 people attend. They appeared well groomed and an average cross-section except that these are single and 90 percent fall within the twenty-five to thirty-five age range. A few older men scattered here and there. The atmosphere of the group reminded me of a five-year reunion of a mixed college sorority and fraternity group. The officers sat in the front at a table and they had reports, etc. ($1,300 in the treasury). They travel to San Francisco, San Diego, Santa Barbara on all sorts of conferences for single Catholics. A few priests in casual dress attend these conferences. There is much booze, cocktail parties, dancing, volleyball, workshops on relevant topics such as sex and structured elections, officers, etc. for Western, Regional, and National this and that.

"This club provides four big dances a year (attendance 500) at the Newporter Inn. Bridge club, volleyball and basketball and softball teams that compete, one social, one cultural and one service project per month. This is the once-a-month business meeting to keep it all going. There was only one clue to this group being Catholic, except for the mention of priests in the slides of the last conference: At the opening and closing protestant-type prayer, they made the sign of the cross.

"The club draws from parishes all over Orange County. Each person attends his own Catholic Church, which may be charismatic or conservative. Once a month they have a 'home mass.' This is officiated by a priest sponser of their group (who is not present at meetings or social functions but who does accompany the overnight trips). A visiting Bishop officiated the last 'home mass.' This 'home mass' idea made *Time* magazine publicity for this group last year.

"They hope to encourage stray Catholics to attend this social organization and then make contact with the Catholic

Church of their choice. The past national president stated that many of their members had not been attending mass but do after they get into the organization.

"The unusual fact of this organization is that the average length of membership is two or three years! They may average six to twelve new members at their once-a-month meeting. These may attend a couple of functions and drop out or join or get redirected to another organization. Those who join usually stay a couple years and attend fairly regularly either most or some activities of their choice. I was aware of the sense of structure, stability, and belonging to a rooted organization.

"There was a strong feeling of pride in their group, in the sense of strong school spirit. People enjoyed one another, knew one another, had jobs and careers outside. There was an air of stability. Of course, there were the usual wallflowers and strays but not a feeling of alienation or apathy or the opposite, socially over-organized. More than anything I got the feeling of being with people who like structure and organization and this club replaces the college Newman club and school activities that they would find difficult to replace. Since drinking, partying, and the like are so much a part of the activities it was not like being with a church group. This club is obviously social.

"This club seems to serve its purpose well: provide a social environment for single Catholic college grads who like being social in college and can continue doing the same sorts of things in the real world with other single Catholic college grads who want the same thing. It eliminates the big trauma of having to sort the Catholics from the non-Catholics for future marriage. Note: Political issues of birth control, abortion, etc., are avoided. If interested, you are directed to the right group."

The Catholic Alumni Club (CAC) has all the signs of a successful organization:

1. Its membership is growing.
2. Members stay involved for years.

3. The group is active, and participation is great.
4. Morale is high; members are enthusiastic.
5. Members like and enjoy each other.
6. Members share the responsibility for running the organization.

In searching for an understanding as to why this church's singles group is so successful, several factors come to mind:

1. First, and I believe most important of all, the CAC group is homogeneous in that its members are Catholic, college graduates, young, middle class, and share common recreational interests. Where one is surrounded by people very similar to oneself, one tends to like the company one is in. When they share the same religious faith, and enjoy doing the same things, they will of course feel a mutual identification and pleasure in each others company. Nor should one underestimate the security assured by associating with persons of the opposite sex but the same faith.

2. The group's social activities are varied and match the interests of the members.

3. This singles group has the benefit of the organizational structure and assistance of a church which is very experienced in developing and supporting church groups.

4. People who are successful like to be together.

5. Catholics have a lifelong background of interacting with other Catholics.

6. Although religion does not tend to be an integral part of CAC meetings, members are never unaware that they share a common faith. Besides the presence of priests and prayers, members are encouraged to attend special masses together.

7. Most CAC members have never been married, and therefore are likely to have more time, money, and energy— and less recent emotional trauma to forget—than is true of recently divorced single persons.

8. Business meetings are infrequent; fun meetings are frequent.

9. Members feel an identification with, and loyalty to, *the organization.*

A *Pew for One, Please*

Despite the flurry of social–recreational activities, it is unlikely that any CAC members forget, or minimize, the fact that the Catholic Alumni Club is a Catholic organization, for Catholics, connected with the Catholic Church. This singles group is, without question, more than just church-sponsored; it is church-*related*. As a college professor, I have sponsored various clubs and societies who had to comply with college rules that each campus organization have a "sponsor." My obligations were few: I merely had to lend my name, and do whatever I chose to do to assist the groups to organize, find housing, recruit members, and plan their activities. In a sense, these groups were professor-sponsored. By contrast, when my old college fraternity, Phi Kappa Tau, decided to found a chapter at the college where I was teaching, they asked for my assistance. I felt that I owed much to the fraternity, and I thought it could render a service to young men. So I became, again, a sponsor—with this difference: I wanted to be involved, to influence. This fraternity chapter became professor-related. In the same way, and for the same reasons, church singles groups such as the Catholic Alumni Club are related to the parent organization. And, like a parent, the church is there on the sideline, lending a hand, making its presence known.

The Professionals

Small organizations of necessity offer no-frill service, which, although not necessarily Spartan, is confined to the delivery of the specific services for which it was created. As the organization grows larger and more affluent, it is able to broaden the range of its activities. It looks for new activities, new markets, new methods of achieving its goals. Once a successful financial base has been established, a core of experienced workers assembled, and new fields identified, the superagency's momentum enables it to move forward to yet another success. Its very size, and its continuing growth, however, can mask weaknesses in its operation. For that reason, giant corporations and institutions often bring in outside consultants to uncover problem areas and to make suggestions for making a good enterprise even better. If this kind of self-examination is not periodically engaged in, the giant eventually falls of its own weight: ". . . it is not so much the *quantity* of experience that matters, as the *quality*. A little experience of the right quality is vastly more important for human happiness than a large amount of experience of the wrong quality. When the quantity begins to outstrip the quality, there is a serious danger of quality going under altogether."[3]

The next church-related singles group that we shall study is based in a church that, in size and influence, is truly a giant. It is the Garden Grove Community Church, hereafter referred to as "Community Church." With a membership of over 10,000, and the ability to reach millions of others through several communication media, this church is one of the pioneers in ministering to singles. My opinions are based on information and impressions gathered during attendance at meetings of its several singles groups by myself and my associate, Arlene Roehm. Members and leaders of this church's singles groups were also very helpful in their willingness to be interviewed and to relate to us their own experiences and opinions.

As one frame of reference by which you can analyze the CRSG, which I shall describe, I would like you to consider a concept presented in the book, *The Split-Level Fellowship*.[4] In it, the author advocates that churches recognize that their membership is "split-level"—that there are two classes of Christians: a small core of consciously committed people with a periphery of an uninvolved majority. The author, Wesley C. Baker, offers several techniques for effecting a more real and harmonious fellowship, suggesting a system of "living cells" or circles of six to ten people. If his theory is correct, perhaps we shall find that some church singles groups constitute a split-level fellowship.

A *Pew for One, Please*

To begin with, Community Church has separate singles groups for different ages. They are:

Pacesetters: 20s
Innovators: 30s
Motivators: 40s
Lamplighters: over 50

The activity schedules of these groups is awesome. So that you might appreciate the number and range of these activities, one month's schedule for each groups follows:

Pacesetters: (50 percent formerly married)

Sunday:	9:30 Worship together
	11:00 Class meeting (lesson, singing, announcements)
	1:00 Brunch in someone's home
	2:30 Volleyball and softball
	5:45 Eventide Service
	7:30 Aftersing in someone's home
Monday:	Meeting in Youth Center
Tuesday:	Open Forum, featuring music
Wednesday:	Volleyball
	Pastor's Class
Thursday:	Board meeting
Friday:	All Family Barbecue
Saturday:	Beach Party
Sunday:	Brunch
	Aftersing
Monday:	Meeting in Youth Center
Tuesday:	"Talk it over"—subject: "The secret of staying in love"
Wednesday:	Volleyball
	Pastor's Class
	LMTC—Special session
Thursday:	Open

Friday:	Open
Saturday:	Brunch
	Alleluia Concert
Monday:	Meeting in Youth Center
Tuesday:	"Talk it Over"

The Innovators are singles in their thirties, up to 85 percent of whom were formerly married. Their schedule approximates that of the Pacesetters, with the addition of such activities as tennis, bridge, potlucks, an ocean cruise, a visit to Enchanted Village, roller skating, dancing, and a family picnic.

The fortyish Motivators, up to 85 percent of whom have been married, add a few more activities, such as serving as Sunday morning hostess, Bible study, a band concert, restaurant dining, and square dancing.

The fifty-and-older Lamplighters, 50 percent of whom are widowed and 50 percent divorced, have a less physically active but equally busy schedule.

Perusal of the programs and recreational activities of these four singles groups in Community Church yields some suggestions for one who wishes to set up singles programs in another church:

1. Offer a great number of planned events, preferably something each day. Some single persons are at temporary points in their life when they need to keep very busy. And, on any given day, when they do need someplace to go and something to do, have something available for them.

2. Schedule a wide range of functions in order to increase the likelihood that each member will find something that will attract and satisfy him or her. Also, a variety will keep interest from waning.

3. Schedule some events in homes.

4. Offer some activities in which the singles' families can participate.

5. Hold some activities in the church's quarters in order to keep the program associated with the church.

6. Do not let the programs become one-sided; functions should be lectures, discussions, parties, athletic games, occasions to dine together, sings, inspirational meetings, planning sessions, outings, and special interest get-togethers.

7. Provide unstructured general meetings where people can shop around for new acquaintances.

The singles administrative structure at Community Church is a marvel of organization and member participation. Its director is a minister who is assigned to singles work full time. It is administered by a young man who is paid to be part time but who is there nearly full time. Each of the four singles groups has several officers, including president, first vice-president, second vice-president, secretary, treasurer, spiritual life chairman, fellowship chairman, brunches chairman, and chairmen of various committees. Each group has a constitution, and most of the individual class programming and planning is administered by each group's officers and members. An executive board consisting of representatives from each group is appointed by the minister-director to serve as a catalyst for ideas, growth, and direction of ministry. As is true in most CRSGs, all elected officers are required to be members of Community Church. Outside groups are thereby prevented from taking over direction of the program. In some CRSGs, officers serve for one year; at Community Church they serve for six months and receive training at a special officer's training retreat.

In a pamphlet distributed to persons interested in how its programs are set up, Community Church explains the financial policies of its singles program. "In order to finance this extensive a ministry, each class receives offerings at its functions, and they carry out various fund-raising projects during the year. At the end of the month, all income is accounted for and distributed in the following way: 50 percent is retained for use by the group, 25 percent is given to the Church, and 25 percent is deposited in a general account for functions that involve all four of our groups. The ministry office is a part of the church budget as are all staff salaries and promotional materials. Each individual group is self-sustaining, and maintains a high level of integrity in their money management." It is clear that Community Church staff keep a firm hand on the policies and practices of its singles groups.

The first Community Church group I attended was the Lamplighters group for those fifty and older. Upon entering, I was warmly greeted, asked to fill out an information form, given a name tag, and then found my way to one of the chairs, which were placed row on row facing the speaker's podium—much like a classroom. Of the forty or so people present, perhaps seven or eight of us were male. All the men moved around greeting the women and frequently conferring with each other on obviously weighty matters. After about thirty minutes of consultations and much peering at papers on the podium, the meeting began with announcements and a resume of recent functions. After several announcements of illnesses and future events, the group had coffee and socialized. One woman with whom I struck up a conversation had been a member for two years—joining shortly after her husband's death.

Lyon: Do you come here often? [I wanted to start out with a snappy, unique question that would capture her attention.]

Lady: Oh, yes. I come to the regular meetings and most of the social events.

Lyon: What is it that attracts you to this group?

Lady: Everybody is so friendly, and there's lots to do. And it's nice to have friends at church—I just can't stand to go places alone. Are you going to join?

Lyon: No, I'm married.

Lady: That's a shame—I mean we could use some more men. What are you doing here then?

Lyon: I've been doing some research on church singles groups. You know, trying to find out which ones are effective—and why.

Lady: Well, you better say good things about this one. It saved my life.

Lyon: It did?

Lady: I said it did, didn't I? When my husband died,
          everyone was so thoughtful and comforting. But
          then everyone went back to their own routines,
          their own lives. I thought I would die of loneliness
          and boredom. I *wanted* to die. And I'm not the
          only one here who feels that this group made a real
          difference—most of us were lonely. Still are; but a
          lot less.

Lyon: Is there anything you would want to change about
          this group?

Lady: More men. The ones we have now are spoiled with
          all the attention they get. And I'd like us to go on
          retreats more, or do something that would—I don't
          know—help me to be more spiritual. And I'd like
          us to get together more with the younger people—
          some of the people here really act their age.

One visit in particular stood out in my mind. It was on one
of the occasions when I observed the youngest singles group,
those in their twenties: After some spirited, guitar-led singing,
a very attractive young woman sat on the floor in the prescribed informed-leader's position, the one that says: "Don't
be intimidated by me; I'm just your run-of-the-mill, garden-
variety, outstanding leader." She began by explaining the
structure of the group. That concisely presented, she
launched into an incredibly minute recitation of the multi-
tudinous activities of the young singles group. After thirty-
five minutes—no exaggeration—she had recited her way
through the schedule from Tuesday through Sunday evening.
"Monday is a free day," she said rather dolefully. "But Monday nights we all come down to the mailroom and stuff en-
velopes with crosses and other religious articles, which the
church sends to the thousands and thousands of people who
support its ministry." The young singles group is one of the
smaller groups in the church. One of its most important functions appears to be the opportunity it provides young people
to learn and practice administrative and leadership skills.

The largest singles group at Community Church is the one whose membership ranges in age from about twenty-five to forty. It is not unusual for 200 or 300 people to attend its Tuesday night meeting. The sex ratio appears to be about three to two in favor of females. The following is a description of what was a typical session—at least for the six Tuesdays we attended:

Most people, especially females, come to their first singles group meeting with a friend (one feels self-conscious, "obvious" on such occasions). After completing the information blank and being stamped with a stick-on name tag, you make yourself less conspicuous by settling into a folding chair. The meeting begins with a few hymns desultorily sung by those few people directly under the songleader's cajoling eyes and hands. One of the group's leaders begins the meeting with a few announcements and then introduces two more officers (regulars and officers are easily identified by their permanent colored plastic name tags). The couple then read from the personal data cards filled out by the newcomers. Each person's introduction is prefaced with a reading of his/her name, occupation, city of residence, and hobbies or interests. The newcomer then stands for inspection and is applauded.

After more announcements, the president introduces the discussion topic for the evening. On my first visit, we completed a self-rating as to how well we lived up to St. Paul's description of love. The general group was then disbanded and everyone sought his own discussion group. People who had been there before seemed to have their preferred discussion group leader.

I looked around for a circle that had an opening in it. The leader, a burly, attractive man of around thirty-five, asked us each to state name, place of residence, and then say what kind of animal we would like to be and why. We then passed an hour of very directive nondirective leadership. No debate was permitted, budding displays of emotion were shut off. When a participant had, in the leader's opinion, gone astray in his/her thinking, the leader would close the interaction with a comment such as, "Well, everybody's entitled to his

opinion; that's what makes us all different from each other."
My own opinion was that the better part of cowardice was to
smile, nod agreeably, and say nothing.

When the subgroup ended, people milled around chatting
and drinking coffee. Many people then met for further socializing at nearby restaurants. Most of them planned to attend
at least one of the activities scheduled during the week. On
one occasion, I had the good fortune to spend two hours over
coffee with the assistant director of the singles programs. My
associate, Ms. Roehm, also spent some hours with him and
the minister in charge.

Our reactions to the Innovators singles group were mixed,
as was true of the participants. Here are the excerpts from
some interviews we conducted over a period of weeks:

A thirty-three-year-old, very pretty woman, who taught
high school. She has been divorced for four years. This was
her second visit to this singles group. Rather standoffish,
seemed glad to have someone to complain to:

Lyon: What brought you here?
Woman: A car.
Lyon: You know what I mean: why do you come here?
Woman: I was looking for something to do, maybe meet
some people.
Lyon: You mean make some new friends?
Woman: Not exactly, I don't especially want any more
women friends. I'd like to meet some guys, maybe
even a guy who doesn't assume you'll go to bed
with him on the first date. Sometimes I think that if
I sent my body out on a date and the rest of me
stayed home nobody would notice—or if they did
they wouldn't mind.
Lyon: Have you found that you meet a different kind of
person here?
Woman: Yeh, in a way. All the guys here aren't
body-shoppers, but I can't say that I've found
many here I'd want to go out with. A lot of people
here are just natural-born wallflowers.

Lyon: How do you feel about the spiritual aspects of the program?

Woman: What spiritual aspects—two hymns and six hugs from people I've just met? Everybody here is too busy relating and making an impression. Its like they're scared that someone will be offended if there is too much concentration on religion. For what you call "the spiritual aspect" they have church services, Bible class, lay minister's classes, Sunday school, and lots of other things. But it's separate from the singles groups as far as I can tell.

Lyon: Do you plan to continue coming here?

Woman: No, I don't think so. There just isn't anything for me here, I guess. Well, maybe there is, but its all so diluted. Maybe I should join a prayer group, a therapy group, and a computer dating service.

My next discussion, over coffee following a Tuesday night meeting, was with a thirty-seven-year-old accountant who had for nine months been a frequent attender of Innovator functions:

Man: How come you're making notes?

Lyon: I'm writing a book on church singles, and this church is said to have one of the biggest and best singles programs.

Man: Then I hope you say something nice 'cause this is a great outfit. I know. I've been coming here for nine months, and its been good for me. I was looking for girls—I can't hack cruising in bars; I'm not good at picking up chicks—but I got interested in the group itself. I hope to be appointed a group leader soon, I hope.

Lyon: Why do you want to be a group leader?

Man: It's kind of like being a member of the in-group. You feel like you're doing something important and—I guess I like the idea of *being* important. There's something to do every day and night of the week if you want.

Lyon: How about religion?

Man: What about it? This is a church isn't it? Most of us go to Sunday service together, and we have a Bible study class and lots of other classes, too. But what I like about this place is they don't overdo the religious approach. We put a lot of emphasis on positive thinking.

Lyon: What would you want to change about this group?

Man: Not much, really; maybe get more good looking chicks.

The third interview, which was typical of several conversations I had with participants of Community Church's singles groups, was with an attractive, slightly pudgy woman, who appeared to be around thirty-four or thirty-five. She had been a member of this singles group for nearly two years. Before, and a number of times during her membership in this group, she had made several short-lived stabs at joining other singles groups. She was a little uneasy about talking to me, although I could not tell whether it was because I was a stranger or because I was asking so many personal questions.

Lyon: Why do you come here?

Woman: Because I have friends here and because there's always something to do if I want to. Its like I have a family. I'm from New Mexico and I was awfully lonely. I don't care whether I date a lot, but I like to do things with other people.

Lyon: You're just naturally gregarious. . . .

Woman: Well, yes; but its no fun to work in a big office all day and then come home and stay there alone. I'm not a mole.

Lyon: Which activities here do you attend?

Woman: Nearly all of them. We keep pretty busy, but it isn't all play. We do a lot of things for the church and for other people. That's what makes us different from other churches; we have a positive attitude about things. So we feel that whatever we try to do will work out OK.

Lyon: Wunnerful, wunnerful. What would you like to change about this organization?

Woman: Less emphasis on dating and more emphasis on fellowship.

No interview, or series of interviews, can capture the complexity of an organization as large and many-faceted as Community Church's singles programs. It is also true that evaluations of a group or an experience, made by someone who has not experienced that group as an insider, cannot hope to fully appreciate the effects that that group has on those who are full participants. On the other hand, just as the insider can more accurately experience and appreciate the positive aspects of the program, so it is true that the nonmember may be in a position to more objectively see the negative aspects of that program.

The Catholic Alumni Club and the Community Church singles program are examples of what I have termed Church-Related Singles Groups (CRSGs). The latter program is often cited as a prototype of what a successful church singles program can, and should, be like. In the following section I shall present what I consider to be the positive and negative (or questionable) aspects of their program. Following that, I shall make some recommendations as to how Community Church's singles programs could be improved.

Merits

1. The church's very size enables it to offer a physical plant, which is more than adequate for the group's activities.

2. Generous support from the church in the form of administrative leadership, finances, publicity, and assistance in planning.

3. A church philosophy that is assertive, innovative, and optimistic.

4. An insistence upon adhering to the church's policies and practices by groups and members.

5. Coordination and interaction between singles groups.

6. Opportunity and encouragement to become involved in the larger church activities.

7. Diversified, frequent, and well-planned activities.

8. Acceptance of prospective members regardless of church affiliation.

9. The opportunity for many people to fill leadership roles.

10. A steady stream of new people with whom to interact.

11. Emphasis upon discussion groups and informal get-togethers.

12. Sophisticated and concerned professional leadership.

13. Attracts and accepts a very heterogeneous membership.

14. Is very accepting and supporting of divorced persons.

15. Close supervision by church staff.

16. A program for training group officers and discussion leaders.

Demerits

One of the paid staff in the singles program at Community Church told me that although anywhere from 200 to 400 people attend the thirty's group each Tuesday night, approximately 75 percent of them will not return. When I commented that to lose 150 or more prospective members each week was a shame, he agreed that it sure was. When I asked if they had done any kind of survey or study to determine why some people returned and others did not, he said no. It appears that having a full house each week diminishes the necessity for increasing the proportion of those first-timers who return. Failure to study or rectify this problem suggests a lack of professional expertise or a "fat cat" attitude.

Group officers, in all age groups, manifest the kind of "special people" personality one associates with high school footballers, cheer leaders, and social leaders. Their interaction with each other and their deportment with ordinary members reminds one of new second lieutenants.

At most regular singles group events, one would find it very difficult to identify the group as being church-related. It is as though everyone were bending over backwards to not force religion on anyone.

Many discussion leaders, who have the most personal—often the only—contact with members, are poorly prepared to function as either group moderators or as examples of warm, understanding friendship. Their training appeared to be superficial and technique oriented; their self-awareness or interpersonal skills varied considerably.

The introductory Tuesday evening meetings are simply too large and too impersonal. The newcomer may appear, spend two hours, and go away only having been said hello to, been introduced at the beginning of the large group session, and introduced oneself in the discussion group. In order to be truly seen, and remembered, one would have to be persistent enough, or desperate enough, to return several times.

The meetings are so structured and paced that there is very little opportunity to relax and feel one's way into the situation.

The groups are so busy-busy that there seems to be little time or interest in quiet interaction, contemplation, or religious experience.

The "clientel" is so heterogeneous that they appear to have little in common other than being single.

With a hundred or so first-timers each night, there is little feeling of continuity or familiarity. Newcomers feel lost.

Data, techniques, and insights of psychology and sociology, which might contribute to the program's improvement, appear to be little used.

The group's constituency appears to be split-level: The majority appear and reappear at activities, but are little involved otherwise. A small minority seems to have based its whole life around the singles group. It has become their career, family, love life, and mission. One wonders how this total involvement affects their attitude toward remarrying.

In summation, at this CRSG, the focus is on statistical success rather than on individual spiritual-emotional growth, on *quantity* at the expense of *quality*.

6

The Church-Dominated Singles Groups

In the two types of church singles groups that we have studied so far, our intent has been to examine to what extent a church influences its singles group and the people in it. The implicit question was, "Is it really a *church* singles group? Or is the church a front for, or a tool of, the singles group with which it is affiliated?" The answers ranged from "quite a bit" to "hardly at all." Now, in the present analysis, the question is reversed: "To what extent is the singles group a front for the church with which it is affiliated?" Not a very nice question is it? But it needs to be asked, for the single person has a right to know, when he first attends a church singles meeting, just what the church expects of him or her.

By "dominated" I mean that the purpose, program, and philosophy of that church's singles program is not to minister to single persons in terms of those problems and needs that are unique to them as *singles* but, rather, to use the singles program as but one more technique for bringing people into the church. Certainly, one cannot criticize a church for evangelizing, but it is a matter of concern when a church is unwilling or unable to minister to individuals in terms of their individual needs and life situations.

Sometimes a church can dominate one of its groups by depriving it of, or failing to help it develop, a sense of identity. One very large church, which we visited and studied, seems guilty of paying only lip service to the need for church programs devoted to ministering to single persons. This church boasts a membership of nearly 10,000, yet it offers but two token singles programs. The younger group number twenty or thirty members who meet on Sunday morning prior to the regular service for a Bible study or to hear a guest speaker discuss the Bible. The one social event of the week is usually attended by ten to fifteen members. The group has a small handful of regulars, while the rest of the membership is quite transient.

This church-dominated singles group (CDSG) also has an older subgroup, who meet on Sunday morning for prayers, songs, Bible study, and a few minutes of socializing. The twenty-five to thirty-five members are mostly regulars who have come to know and like each other. On Saturday nights they have some kind of informal social function. Both of these singles groups spend approximately 90 percent of their time together in some kind of religion-related activity. Their relationship to the church does not seem to be at all defined in terms of their being single persons in a singles group.

A person looking for immediate sharing, friendliness, and expressions of affection would not be disappointed by these two singles groups. Strangers freely express love toward each other, very personal experiences are related without self-consciousness, and testimonies of religious experiences are enthusiastically described, as one would expect in a church that considers itself fundamental and charismatic. There is an air of excitement in the air; spontaneous praying out loud, cries of despair, altar calls, miraculous healings, anguished confessions, professions of love, reaching out to one another as common recipients of grace—all this is stimulating, perhaps satisfying, to one who is alone. This church, it would appear, conceives of its ministry to singles as being a chance to end their loneliness by bringing them closer to Jesus—although not necessarily closer to each other.

Several visits to other "fundamentalist-charismatic" churches confirmed our theory that when two churches share a common theology and personality, then that communality will be discernible in the groups that the two churches house. In this study, we moved from a church of 10,000 to a church of 200. On our last visit there, this is how the evening went:

At 7:30 P.M. the meeting began with a prayer led by a part-time minister. There were sixteen of us there—about ten were of high school or college age, and six of us ranged from thirty-five to fifty or so. The songs seemed, at first, rather like children's songs—simple and repetitive. By the third song, I found myself having as much fun as were the others. The music was up-beat and lent itself easily to harmonizing. Three novice guitarists competed for the right to lead the singing. At the end of half an hour, everyone was smiling and relaxed.

The minister selected a Bible passage, read it aloud, and then explained it for about thirty minutes. Every few minutes the sermon was punctuated by ejaculations of "Praise the Lord; thanks be to God; Amen; yea brother; hallelujah;" and "right on, brother." The evening's main event was next. A very shy young Chicano then rose to deliver his prepared testimony. His awkward yet moving talk detailed how he had lost his wife, baby son, job, and friends when he joined this church and "accepted Jesus Christ as my personal savior." The audience was moved by his story and his sincerity; their agrement and encouragement were expressed in fervent cries of "Praise Jesus!" It was obvious that this young man was considered to be a modern martyr. During and after his address, the other singles group members expressed joy over his having been saved from a life of ignorance and sins. Their approbation and reinforcement seemed very important to him.

Finally, there came the Bible study period, in which the group discussed spiritual healing in terms of its constituting proof of the power of Jesus and the gifts of the Spirit. When two visitors began a line of thought concerning suggestibility, psychosomatic medicine, and the power of the person, three older members of this CDSG became very aroused and aggressive in their disagreement. At this point the minister announced that it was time for coffee and cookies. By this time, this writer had blown his cover as a single person and then unmasked as a psychologist-professor. Two of the three older members then devoted themselves to convincing me and another guest that unless one accepted literally every word in the Bible, one's soul was lost and hell was inevitable. My purpose, and that of the other guests, had been to see what this group could offer a single person. The answer was clear: salvation. Singleness clearly was not any more germane to this group's real purpose than was one's geographical origin, height, or taste in ice cream.

Miss Roehm later conducted an interview with the pastor of this church. His interest and perception of single people was almost identical with those opinions and attitudes expressed by the pastors of two other churches, which were similar in their philosophy and theology. He expressed the belief that singles need fellowship and support in order for them to fight temptation and loneliness. Single people, especially, are faced with desires and opportunities that could lead to sinful behavior, which would place their souls in mortal jeopardy. He also expressed his belief that single people should get together in church singles groups so that they might mutually help each other to lead a Christian life. He did not cite any other reasons for supporting a singles group. All that one could infer was that since single people were younger than married people, and lonelier, and would feel uncomfortable in a nonsingles group, why there ought to be a group for single people.

Summary: I would define a church-dominated singles group as one in which the primary emphasis is upon ministering to the members' spiritual needs to the exclusion of other needs, such as the psychological, emotional, recreational-social, educational, and practical problems of divorce and living alone. With few exceptions, the programs and purposes of this kind of group would be applicable to most other of that church's groups. Essentially, then, the CDSG is not really a singles group in the fullest sense of the word, and such groups are dramatically different from other church singles groups I have studied. Since I did not encounter this kind of singles group in any churches other than those which might be described as "fundamentalist, evangelical, or charismatic," perhaps therein lies the explanation as to why the focus in their singles groups seems to have less to do with their communality as singles than with their spiritual life.

At the CDSG, I was struck by the enthusiasm and fluency with which the members communicated their joy over having been "saved" and their delight at being with each other. They appeared convinced that for them loneliness, pain, and confusion have been permanently put to route by Jesus and the Bible. There is little uncertainty here; nor is there much interest in self-analysis other than in removing the roadblocks to repentence and salvation. Very little tolerance is manifested for different theological beliefs or life-styles. Thus, the membership is homogeneous and mutually reinforcing.

The character and personality of the CDSG is very similar to the kind of conservative church that of recent years has far outstripped the more liberal churches in increase of membership. Dean M. Kelley has specified some of the maxims that such churches teach their members:

1. Do not confuse this church with other beliefs, loyalties, practices, nor should one consider them equal or compatible with ours.
2. Make high demands on members.
3. Do not consent to, encourage, or indulge any violations of our standards of belief or behavior.
4. Do not keep silent about it, apologize for it, or let it be as though it made no difference in their behavior or in their relationships with other organizations.[1]

What do people find in the CDSG? From what I was able to see—and this was true in the several we studied—the members of these groups are usually young people on a quest for meaning, security, and joy. A principal speaker at a national charismatic Catholic confluence opined that its adherents are finding "expressions of righteousness and love and joy and peace breaking out to which they are attracted. I think the heart of the thing is really what Jesus prayed for at the Last Supper—that we would be of one mind and one heart and that we would love one another the way he loves us." The speaker added that, "the young are attracted to it. Conservatives are attracted to it, clergy, religious—it's a whole cross-section of God's people."[2] What the CDSG offers, I believe, is a concentrated dose of a strictly defined dogma to those single people whose spiritual and emotional needs can best be met in an emotional, rigid, impersonal, and religiously sure atmosphere. For a time, many people are satisfied with what they are getting out of this kind of group. And there is no question but that these groups consider man's spiritual needs to have precedence over other personal needs. That is about all the good that I can say about the church-dominated singles group.

On the negative side, I have several concerns about the CDSG:

1. Single persons are not considered as a unique group with problems unique to their single state.
2. Very little emphasis is placed on self-growth through self-understanding.
3. The "sharing" that takes place is not really personal or intimate. Rather, it resembles more a kind of mutual self-congratulating and inciting of feelings of relief and joy over having escaped the fate of outsiders. And confession and testimony are a part of, but not synonymous with, true intimacy and interpersonal feeling.
5. A prospective member who does not wish to put aside his or her concerns about the problems of being single would be dissatisfied.
6. A prospective member who is not yet ready to commit himself to a new system of beliefs or a radically revised style of life would feel misunderstood or rejected.
7. Groups that offer instant love would be met with

suspicion and unease by those whose standards for love and acceptance are more demanding.

8. Instant cures—and many people profess to have experienced them—are not likely for those who are not ready to trust completely in the belief that God will take care of everything.

9. Such groups can, inadvertently or not, force people to repress rather than to suppress, and to suppress rather than to express—to a neurotic degree.

10. People seeking a continuous series of spiritual highs can become spiritual junkies.

11. Social activities in CDSGs often are underemphasized. So, the spiritual experience can also become the emotional, the interpersonal, even the recreational experience.

12. Because of church overcontrol this kind of group, over a period of time, makes members who were merely similar into people who are undifferentiated as persons.

7

The Church-Integrated Singles Group

The three criteria that must be met if a singles group is to be considered a church-integrated singles group (CISG) are:

1. That the group be considered as an integral part of the general church's functioning, both administratively and philosophically. This means that the CISG is given the assistance, respect, and importance accorded to other church groups such as: study groups, Sunday school teachers, choir, altar guild, women's group, prayer group, stewardship committee, couples' group, etc. Otherwise, the same feelings of rejection, inferiority, and impotence that society activates in the single person will also be created in the singles group.

2. That the individual singles group member be an active participant in another of a church's general activities, preferably in the church that houses the singles group.

3. That the group's programs, purposes, and "personality" provide the kind of interpersonal spiritual experience that engenders in the members attitudes of trust, sharing, affection, support, and self-growth.

If the above factors do not characterize a CISG, then the group can only be considered as another one of the church's outreach ventures, such as foreign missions, sponsoring senior citizens' hot meals programs, boy and girl scout clubs, and assistance given to civil rights movements. There can be no doubt that the church's history and self-concept impel it to offer assistance and success to those in need. It is true, however, that other than in terms of the benefits accruing from being generous and loving, such as enhancement of one's character and self-concept, church *aid* programs are unidirectional: one gives and the other receives. (The giver tends to like himself better, and the receiver tends to like himself less.) Professional givers, such as counselors and ministers, are aware of the intense desire, or need, that many people have to give something in return. If this cannot be, then the relationship remains unidirectional rather than reciprocal, hierarchical rather than horizontal. The church singles group, which is only "sponsored" or "related," cannot enjoy the benefits of being "part of the family." Instead, such groups can only be considered charity cases, who receive some part of what the "family" has left over.

Not every beneficiary, however, is strongly motivated to repay its benefactor. Many nonintegrated church singles groups seem quite content with being the recipients of church donations of physical plant, reputation, organizational skill, money, staff, and drawing power. Certainly many individuals are quite contented to receive whatever charity or assistance they can obtain from other persons or groups. I do not believe that the church is being constructive to the persons or groups themselves when it conveys to them that passive dependency or self-centeredness are acceptable—not just as temporary conditions in times of need—but as a way of life. That church, or some church, has a right to expect something in return for its compassion and generosity.

If one believes that the church has a mission to succor to all those in need, then we must ask why should the church not administer medicare, social security, social service, mental health, unemployment, child protection, education, and all other programs devoted to the care and protection of human beings. Fortunately, we have long since rejected such a philosophy. This being true, it would seem reasonable that the church would generally involve and invest itself in housing and nurturing only those programs intimately related to its mission as the church conceives it. If such a self-concept justifies work in areas such as the "civil problems" listed above, then I believe that the *manner* in which the church participates should personify what the church stands for. If a church teaches respect and love for others, then it must personify these qualities and dedicate itself to teaching and expecting such qualities in those to whom it ministers. Germane to the subject of this book: A church singles group should be a setting wherein mutual respect and love are basic characteristics of the interactions between members, and between members and the church. There *are* some church singles groups that meet this standard. They are the church integrated singles groups (CISGs).

The ambiance in the meeting room of this upper middle-class Presbyterian church was noticeably different from that of other church singles groups we had visited. There were about twenty people in the room, and it was obvious that they were not strangers to each other. One sensed an at-easeness and familiarity that is more likely to be found in a family gathering than in a meeting of persons whose lives interact only occasionally outside of their weekly meetings. As one attractive, outgoing young woman phrased it: This singles group is a place to pray together, sing together, and be together—just like a family. I look forward to coming each week for the sharing, where people care about you." The young man she was talking with added that "It's a relief to have a place to go where everybody isn't cruising or just trying to fill up time. I do my share of chasing women, and sometimes I do things just to keep busy, but this place isn't like that—we really enjoy being with each other."

Although it has a few visitors and newcomers from time to time, this CISG has a core group, which has been in regular attendance for a year or more. Visitors tend not to return unless they are looking for relationships rather than activities

77

and a place to meet prospective dates. A typical Friday night meeting includes singing and guitar playing (of a surprisingly high quality), a lot of one-on-one conversation, an hour or more of discussion of a Bible passage, and a holding of hands during a twenty- or thirty-minute prayer session at the end. The conversations and discussions are lively, replete with a few facts interspersed with personal opinion and personal reminiscences. An observer would have no doubts but that what holds these single people together is, primarily, their interest in religion and, secondarily, their pleasure in being with each other. A beautiful, twenty-five-year-old high school teacher explained that: "This is a neat time to just let your hair down; its like a refueling station here. I can relax instead of meeting 'worldly expectations.' Seek ye the Kingdom of God," she declared. "If I look first to the Lord, he will supply me with the relationships I need."

"That's right," said the clean-cut young realtor next to her. "Christ makes a difference in relationships." When the group moved into a discussion of Christ's love and how it could be a part of the love expressed between a man and a woman, there developed the kind of earnest, open expression of thoughts and feelings that one expects to find in a therapy group. The emphasis, however, was upon knowing and understanding each other within a Christian frame of reference. Somehow, what happened that evening was, from a psychologist's perspective, therapeutic without being therapy. That this delicate balance could be maintained was due in great part to the leadership of the man in charge of the singles program.

Social psychologists know that one means of coming to understand the character and personality of a group is to study that group's leader(s). Ministers, teachers, psychologists, military officers, and coaches mold and model—whether they intend to or not. Such seems to be true of this singles group. The leader, Steve, is a good-looking, athletic young man, who has completed advanced graduate studies in psychology and counseling. His good looks, charm, and sophistication do not prepare one for his rather diffident style of leadership. The group's unconcern, even disinterest, in each other as prospective dates is highlighted by Steve's statement that "Here in this group we get the chance to get needs met without having to date; we're free to love one another without the pressure of getting into roles. Steve's, and the group's, almost asexual interrelationships are described, and justified, by statements such as: "Our love of Jesus will be evident by the way we are with one another." And, "Faith in the fact that God loves you makes loving others more possible. Having this faith, we singles can get together like a family."

This CISG would be, and should be, considered one of the more successful and effective singles groups. Its members are very happy with it, its church is proud of it, and other singles groups envy it. If the purpose of churches is to assist people to feel and express love toward one another and toward God, then this singles group can truly be termed a *church* singles group. As a means of explaining this CISG's effectiveness, the following factors can be singled out:

1. The members would generally be considered "winners." Young, attractive, educated, socially confident, with a consistent, high-level value system.

2. The membership is homogeneous; they can identify with, understand, and accept each other.

3. They are in emphatic agreement that what brings, and holds, them together is the fact that they are single persons who are seeking a religious experience.

4. There is little if any of the tension usually created by dating-mating behavior.

5. The participants want a "family" type of experience.

6. Because the group is composed of a small number of people, who attend regularly over a period of many months, there is a continuity and intimacy that would otherwise not be possible.

7. The emphasis is upon enjoying each other rather upon a multiplicity of outside activities.

8. The members take great pleasure in cooperative activities such as singing, Bible study, and sharing of personal experiences.

9. The impact of their weekly meeting is not diluted by

during-the-week activities. This also prevents the development of cliques.

10. The leader, who is a member of the church staff, is ex-
ceptionally qualified for his job. Besides his obvious positive
qualities, Steve has been trained as a professional leader. His
graduate training as a counselor gives him the kind of expertise that is needed to weld individuals into a group, and to
make that group experience psychologically and spiritually
beneficial.

11. Since members either leave or are added to the group
only occasionally, the group's "personality" remains consistent. This is true—as it can be true in other groups that
have a slow turnover, such as fraternities and therapy
groups—even though at the end of a year or two there
remains not a single person who was in the group at its in-
ception.

Some possible disadvantages of a church singles group
such as the one described above are:

1. Since the members are very homogeneous in backgrounds, personal characteristics, and what they want from
the group, many prospective members would not fit comfortably into this group.

2. The members' attitudes and beliefs can become narrow
and rigid.

3. As a consequence of their being so pleased with their
group, the members individually and collectively may
become smug.

4. Having a substitute family, they may be less motivated
to seek or create a love life or family of their very own.

5. Because they generally see each other only at those
Friday night meetings that they attend, the members may
never really have to know or relate to each other in "real
life."

A church-integrated singles group, which is similar but yet
quite different from the CISG just evaluated is described in

Christian Life by Janet Fix, who chronicles the birth and development of the singles group at the Church of the First Assembly God in North Hollywood, California. Explaining the need for church singles groups, she says:

> Singles have become neither fish nor fowl in the Christian world. Most churches relegate the singles to their own little corner of the church, isolating them from the mainstream of events, feeling satisfied that there is a "singles fellowship" for them until they are married. If there aren't enough singles to form a "singles group," they are either put in the youth department (if they are anywhere near being young) or they are given a Children's Sunday School class to teach, or they are just left out of the Christian education program of the church.[1]

In one of the few statements I have encountered about the responsibility of the singles themselves to *do* something about their religious isolation, she admits that,

> In all honesty, I can't put all the blame for this segregation on the church, because singles have a tendency to be inward in their thinking and lifestyle. After all, many have been single for a long time and have had to fend off questions and well-meaning set-ups for blind dates from anxious friends and family. Singles who are divorced are subject to a different set of queries and suspicions, so it doesn't take long for sensitivity and defensiveness to build. Many singles acquire chips on their shoulders that are hard to knock off. Some singles seem to pamper and nurture those chips, too, only to increase the gulf between one another and the rest of the body of Christ."

Miss Fix's candor is refreshing, for, like most individuals and groups who feel themselves to be discriminated against, singles (individually or within a group) often are more devoted to demanding acceptance than they are in evaluating what they need do to *deserve* and *effect* their integration into the church body. And when they are given assistance they will often huddle together in the security of their common uniqueness. This kind of in-grouping serves only to widen the gulf between them and the larger group to whom they are looking for acceptance. Her own group's approach was much more realistic:

> The officers of the class met together and prayed and talked about what part we wanted to take in this large family of God—if any. We had to decide if we were willing to drop the walls we had built and make ourselves vulnerable; willing to step out of the security of our familiar idiosyncracies into the larger unknown. We knew we couldn't be a healthy branch of the body if we continued in our own self-centered interests, so we made ourselves available to the staff of the church, willing to be used, no matter how menial the task.

This CISG made its members available to serve at table for a Senior Citizens dinner, attended regular church services *en masse*, participated heavily in Missions Emphasis Month, working with a struggling small county church several miles away, inviting church leaders to their meetings, doing anything they could conceive of as proving their desire and right to be considered an integral part of the church. One of the tangible results of this CISG's mature acceptance of their own responsibility for changing others' perceptions of them is that singles group members now serve on this church's Christian Education Board, World Outreach Board, Finance Committee, and Evangelism Committee.

Miss Fix, who provided the initial concept and force behind The Single Saints, as they call themselves, concludes her narrative by saying:

> We've come a long way, but we still have a long way to go. We have grown from the small, lonely Single Saints, to a thriving group of nearly seventy every week, and

we're still growing. But now we're not just a body of singles set apart as lonely orphans. We're part of a much larger family of God. I believe the most important thing we have accomplished is the awareness on all sides of the need for fellowship and ministry. We singles need to feel that we belong to a family—and its happening.

For the members of this church singles group, their church membership is not all work. They plan, and enjoy, a range of social activities which is limited only by their religious beliefs. Their goal, and it is one that I believe should be approximated by other church singles groups, has been to become an *integral* part of the church body. This goal undoubtedly is more easily realized in those denominations and churches that emphasize a close, during-the-week involvement with church activities.

Summary

The church integrated singles group described above embodies the same qualities of *agape*, emphasis upon fellowship rather than socializing, and a deep interest in Christianity and their own spiritual needs as was true of the Presbyterian CISG previously described. The former church, however, would be a better bet for those singles who have a strong commitment to active participation in the daily affairs of the church. They would, probably, be less motivated by the prospects of meeting people to date. Like the Catholic singles groups, the Assembly of God singles group members would have the assurance of meeting people whose religious beliefs and practices are similar to their own.

The most striking feature of the singles group described by Janet Fix is its willingness to face, and to fight, the prejudice and ignorance characteristic of married people's attitudes toward single people. Too, their response to this discrimination would be described as *assertive* rather than aggressive. This is crucial, for an aggressive style can be interpreted as saying "*You* are wrong;" while an assertive stance states: "I expect to be treated fairly and considerately." And, rather than passively wait for a dole, this CISG set itself to *earning* acceptance and integration into the church body. In return these singles were accorded the entrance and participation that is usually denied singles groups. Perhaps a part of their success with the general church members lies in their insight into their own tendencies to be defensive and self-pitying. By refraining from withdrawing or projecting blame, they were able to forestall the counterhostility that usually is aroused when a person or group accuses another of being prejudiced. Nonetheless, it must be recognized that this singles group, and others like it, might not be appropriate for persons who are not committed or even interested in becoming heavily involved in a particular church. Too, this singles groups' close interaction with its church would probably preclude prospective membership by a single person who either belongs to another church or who does not yet have an interest in joining *any* church.

This look at two church-integrated singles groups clearly has shown that singles groups can be created as integral parts of the church and still retain the individuality of the persons, the group, and the church. More important, within this kind of group structure the church can become an integral part of the person.

8

Business as Usual

The singles business is big business. As has been true in so many other areas of human concern and endeavor, the church's role as shepherd and counselor is in danger of being usurped by more aggressive, sophisticated, and commercial agencies. Singles bars, social clubs, apartment complexes, travel agencies, and recreation hucksters lure single people with their promises of companionship, fun, romance, and activity. Advertisements like the following run in every metropolitan newspaper:

> *Single?*
> If you're dissatisfied with singles bars, dances, and other "meet markets," yet still want to expand your social life, then it's time you find out about _____.
> Through _____ you can meet other selective, sincere singles who, like you, are looking for more than superficial encounters and role-playing.
> _____ is a totally new concept that offers you the quickest, easiest, and most effective way yet devised to make new friends, whether for dating or just good company. You can meet one to one, at our unique private parties, dances, theater and dinner outings, sporting events, personal growth and travel experiences, etc.
> Thousands of active members throughout the Greater Los Angeles area.

If what many thousands of people need is a place to meet new friends, why not the church? Singles groups that are church sponsored or church related would seem to be an ideal setting where people can find and enjoy each other.

Every week I receive one or more brochures advertising counseling—mutual support programs for single persons. One of them describes its services as follows:

> Suddenly seeing themselves as separate individuals after years of identification as part of a couple, many men and women find themselves critically assessing their personal attributes, confused over new goals and directions, and wanting to share this experience with others who are facing the same problems of transition and change.
>
> Those who have experienced the termination of a long-time relationship with another person are familiar with the feeling of shock and loneliness, the anger, the guilt, and the urge to rush too fast into the security of another relationship. Participants are encouraged to share their feelings and help each other in dealing with them.

As a professional psychologist, I am relieved to find that there are agencies and groups to which I can refer people who are in the midst of struggling to make a new life—or of deciding whether it is worthwhile or possible to go on living. So often, when confronted in my office by a man or woman who is experiencing the almost unbearable grief and/or anxiety resultant from being widowed or divorced, I have wished that I were a physician so that I could write a prescription that might make them feel better, or a minister who might offer them meaning and hope, or, best of all, a friend who could be with them in their dark hours. For years I have been involved with treating people who find themselves alone and apparently unwanted. I have recently authored a book on the subject.[1] Ideas and facts are helpful, but when one is alone and lonely, the only answer is *another person*—preferably several other persons with whom one can feel secure, understood, and loved. The church-integrated groups are especially appropriate as a place where single people—whether they are feeling too much or too little—can find help and hope.

There are other single persons whose primary investment in life is in discipleship and service to their church. As has been noted many times—but only recently—this kind of Christian single has had to face a narrow-minded suspiciousness on the part of married people. Well, our "closet" Christian singles are in the open and they are making themselves known. As one such single puts it, "What God really cares about is not my marital status, but what I am doing with what I have and how I relate to my fellow beings." And ". . . God's plans for a single person are just as important, just as carefully and lovingly thought up as his plans for married person."[2]

For many people, being single does not, in and of itself, constitute a problem. They are either contented with being single for the time being, or they may have concluded that they do not wish to marry. These people are not asking to be accepted in spite of being single, or because of being single, but *regardless* of whether or not they are single. They are making the valid point that being single is not something that needs to be excused or explained. In fact, single people can justifiably claim that they may well be able to give more of themselves to the church than can married people. One writer, in strong response to the prejudice and ignorance characterizing many writers' perceptions of single people's usefulness to the church said:

> But don't tell your pastor that the average church attendee in the U.S. donates $154 a year, while the average single adult will deposit $280 in the offering plate. If the pastor knew this, he might get excited and start to work among the young adults for purely financial reasons.
>
> Also, don't tell him the average single adult hates to sit at home at night looking at four walls or at the television screen. Don't tell him young careerists want to act, plan, and get involved.

If he knew this, he might *use* you to visit the sick, work in a settlement house, invite prospective members, serve on church committees, write and edit the church paper, take care of bulletin boards, write plays, supervise children's programs, or plan and direct church-wide recreation and picnics. His motive might be to enlarge his parish rather than to minister to people.[3]

If the question is, "Does the church need the single person?" then the answer is an emphatic "Yes!" We know that single persons number at least one-third of the present church population. What proportion they might represent were churches to more effectively prosyletize single members, or were it to deal with them with more understanding and appreciation than it now does, we could only guess. The church needs single people. It needs their energy, money, time, love, and their unique potential for commitment.

Do single people need the church? Again, the answer is an unqualified "Yes!" Many single people are suffering greatly *because* they are single. Many other single people are not in conflict or unhappy about being single—they may not be in conflict or unhappy at all. But they need, could benefit from, a church involvement just as would a married person. In human relationships, it is usually the one in greater need who asks for something from the one in the stronger, less needy position. But in order to ask, one must admit to being in need of the other's love and strength. This is hard to do, and many of us will do without rather than to ask. The church, its members, its ministers are in the stronger position. I believe that it is up to them to reach out to the single person rather than standing back.

There is much that the church can do to bring single persons into the fold. Many individual churches have made a start. Some denominations appear to be awakening to the possibilities for service to, and rewards from, the singles population. For example, the California–Nevada Conference of the United Methodist Church has issued the following Singles Manifesto:

Singles call upon the church to be aware of the many single persons who are in the church and community, together with the varieties of singleness (never married, divorced, widowed) . . . and

(1) To recognize singleness as a legitimate life style and acceptable status.

(2) To affirm persons who are single through choice or circumstance by structuring church activities and programs to be inclusive rather than exclusive (not family or age-oriented exclusively).

(3) To develop within the life of the church support structures uniquely designed to meet the needs of single persons and/or one-parent families.

(4) To be aware that single persons need to FEEL and BE a part of the total ministry of the church.

(5) To be aware that single persons are ready to share their gifts and talents as a part of the total ministry of the church.

(6) To recognize the injustice and inequities that single persons experience in economic, social, political areas of life and become involved as an agent of change. (Example: Taxes, credit, leisure activities, and societal attitudes.)

(7) To develop a theology which deals with divorce as a fact of life and recognize divorced persons and one-parent families resulting from divorce as acceptable persons who need love and support.

(8) To become aware of cultural stereotypes which tend to assume marriage as the only acceptable life style. (Example: "When are you going to settle down?" "It's too bad a nice person like you isn't married." "Too bad about your divorce; what did he/she do?" "Aren't you married yet?" "Come to the potluck; we'll find someone to sit with you."

This singles manifesto is but one more statement, or demand, which heralds the end of majority rule. In fact, at times it is difficult to *find* a majority. Nearly everybody, it seems, is a member of some minority group. In my role of psychological consultant I am often told that I couldn't possibly be of help to some person or group inasmuch as I am not black, alcoholic, female, born-again, homosexual, paroled, young, old, poor, drug-addicted, psychotic, single, etc., etc. Finally, there not being a minority group that would have me, I consoled myself by deciding that I therefore constituted a minority. I now belong; I can even feel discriminated against; but I need to add many new members if my minority group is going to achieve power against the majority. Then I can start demanding fair treatment from the majority—I may even decide to join them. Of course, when I do that I shall no longer be a discriminated-against minority.

As has been pointed out already, single persons number as much as one-third of the church-going population. They can hardly be considered a small minority group. Besides, a very high percentage of the church majority group (married) will, through divorce or death of a spouse, become members of the minority (singles) group. These single people are calling for full acceptance into the church community. They may appreciate and enjoy the church's efforts to improve their social life, but no longer will they tolerate the kind of condescending treatment that has been their lot in the past. True, many single people will not remain single for long, and too many of them have no conscious desire to participate in church activities. What is needed is for church leaders and members to develop an awareness and appreciation of single persons as, basically, just people. The single may have some special needs, but who hasn't? These needs can be attended to, and satisfied, without making a special case out of the single person who sees him/herself as a person who is single, not as a single.

In short, what I am advocating is that the church would be more successful in its singles work if it concentrated more on needs and less on trying to figure out what it can do to help *those people*. We have seen that being single can pose special problems such as loneliness, financial, and child-rearing concerns, feelings of guilt, pessimism, and self-doubting, but it does not alter the fact that we are dealing with persons. Even their "special" problems and needs are not really unlike those which beset un-single people.

If singles are really just people and if their needs are not unique to them, is there reason to "single" them out for special attention from the church? My reply would be yes, but with a change in emphasis. Rather than focus on "problem people" or "people with problems," we might more efficiently and effectively be of service if we were to look more carefully at the *problems* of people. For example, not all single people are unhappy, lonely, neurotic, or in a spiritual dilemma. If, like the church-sponsored singles groups, we offer a meeting place and impetus to those single people who are lonely, we shall have done all that is wanted by many single persons. In like fashion, the three other kinds of church singles groups I have cited will satisfy the needs of many single persons. My bias for the church-integrated singles group as being the most valuable kind of church singles group has, I would imagine, been obvious to the reader. My bias is based on my contention that the CISG, first, avoids the error of concentrating on either end of the social-spiritual continuum and, second, because it creates an atmosphere in which people can be helped with their *problems*. These problems can include the whole spectrum of human existence. What is important—what is the essence of the true church group—is that the CISG allows and encourages the development of trust, affection, self-growth, openness, love, acceptance, support, and generosity among the members.

By attending to people's psychological, emotional, practical, and spiritual problems, we are not deemphasizing their uniqueness or humanness, only their singleness. After all, many married people are lonely, depressed, socially inhibited, spiritually dry, and inactive in church affairs. If a church is dedicated to assisting single persons who have intrapersonal and interpersonal needs, then it should look further to the general church population. They, too, could benefit from a program and environment that espouses and encourages love of self and of others. I cannot help but fantasize what it could mean to a church if it used its singles program as a test group from which it might learn how to improve its other programs and groups. For this kind of learning experience to be valuable it would, of course, have to be designed and administered in cooperation with the church administration and lay leaders. Far too many church singles groups are either considered as appendages or possessions of the general church.

There is a great need for church involvement with single persons, and the results can be mutually beneficial. But if a church involves itself in singles work from a base of ignorance, paternalism, or a laissez-faire philosophy, neither side will benefit. Singles work, like youth programs, evangelism, education programs, senior citizens activities, couples groups, spiritual healing, and Bible study, requires a serious, professional committment. What I mean by "professional" will be explained in the next chapter.

9

The Who, How and Why of Church Singles Groups

This is an age of specialization and status consciousness. Garbage collectors have become sanitation engineers, mailmen are letter carriers, janitors are building superintendents, housewives are homemakers. It seems that when we discriminate against some group, we refer to its members by an appellation, which identifies them as inferiors. Nowadays, not only is it not polite to be prejudiced, but the objects of our prejudice are refusing to accept their former status. One sign of their assertiveness and self-respect is their insistence that they not be referred to in derogatory terms. Homosexuals are gays, negroes are blacks, old people are senior citizens, the mentally retarded are developmentally disabled and bachelors, spinsters, old maids, divorcées and widows have become single persons. Even being identified as "unmarried" is considered a put down; it is a statement of what one is not—so we are asked to refer to females as "Ms." Since it is true that demeaning labels have dynamic power, when we call someone by a derogatory term he or she tends to feel inferior, and we tend to respond to them as though they were what we have called them; it takes time before the new labels and attitudes take effect. Until then, the labelers and the labeled need to be alert to well-meaning but naïve attempts to "help" those in need by setting up programs for them. The need for intelligent, sophisticated, serious planning is nowhere more apparent than in church programs for single persons.

Who?

We cannot take for granted that if we decide to help some group that that group wants our help, or even that we are capable of helping them. And, who is "them"? Should a church consider creating a singles program, it first must decide *which* singles it is interested in:

1. Young, teen-age singles who live at home?
2. College and part-college age singles who live away from home?
3. The prespinster-age single persons in their thirties?
4. Divorcées?
5. Widows and widowers?
6. Senior citizens?
7. Religiously committed singles who may well not marry?
8. Homosexuals?
9. Those who go to church?
10. Any single person who happens to show up?

Too often, well-meaning philanthropic or altruistic programs fail because they have not defined precisely their target population. Most churches will not have a large enough sample of all of the possible singles subgroups to make it feasible for the church to mount a broad campaign to service all single persons. If it should elect to jointly sponsor a singles program between two or more churches it can broaden its approach, but at the risk of diluting or perverting its goals. In most churches there will be a bimodel distribution of single people, with one group who are in their thirties and forties who are divorced and another group forty-five and up who are widowed or divorced. These two groups offer the best odds for giving a favorable response to a singles program. Singles in their twenties and those in their sixties are often already involved in one or more age—and interest-group—activities. Even so, at both ends of the life cycle there is an unusually high interest in peer group activities and relationships. When two or more churches cosponsor a singles group, it would be well for them to do so with a church whose values and traditions will not be in conflict with the other church's. If two ministers or their lay leaders are in disagreement about such activities as dancing, drinking, smoking, sexual behavior, or if they differ markedly in their beliefs about such issues as divorce, remarriage, prayer, birth control, or what constitutes a Christian life, this discord will spill over into the singles program. Church-sponsored or church-related singles groups do not run as much risk of interchurch conflict as do the church-integrated and church-dominated groups.

Generally, the more homogenous the groups, the more successful the programs will be. Factors to be considered are age, religious beliefs, social class, education, income, recreational interests, and what they hope to gain from participating in a singles group. If singles group members do not have a lot in common, they will be as disinclined to interact with each other as they would be outside the singles group. Should a church decide to serve single persons who are not members of that church, it should make it clear from the beginning what its rules, limitations, expectations, and goals are. Thus, before long, that church singles group would have a method of operation, and reputation, that would attract people who would be comfortable in that singles group. People would then self-select, or deselect themselves as potential members of that group.

Larger churches, which have the financial and administrative resources necessary to offer a wide range of services to a heterogenous population, many of whom have little or no interest in religion or the church, can effectively create and manage what might be termed a funnel program.

Community Church's singles program is an example of how successful this type of program is for me. Community Church maintains an open-door policy toward all singles, whether they be bachelors, divorcées, widows, young, old, church members, atheists, agnostics—all are welcome. This broad stream of newcomers is first narrowed down into age groups. Within this age group, which meets regularly and frequently, the members sort themselves into cliques and interest or activity groups. Ultimately, many of these people who came in as "singles shoppers" will have begun paying back some of what they have been given; they will be contributing time, money, energy, and love to the church. At this point they will have left the general group of "single persons" and earned the designation of "Christian."

Again, it is mperative that a church that proposes to foster the creation of a singles program first set itself to answering the question of which singles are to be served. Unless interpersonal relationships are not intended to be a focal point or goal, a program that attempts to give a little bit to everybody will soon find that it is giving nothing to anybody. A more realistic approach would be to begin with a more modest program, designed to be maximally effective with a small group, or range, of single persons. When that goal is realized, *then* is the time to extend the program to one more additional segment of the singles population. In that fashion, the church will be able to personify the love, concern, and generosity it teaches. Taken slowly, external growth may be slower but internal growth will be faster.

HOW?

Regardless of which one thought of it first, a new church singles group has as parents a pastor and one or more of his parishioners. Sometimes singles groups are "just born" without anyone being sure when casual get-togethers became scheduled meetings. This is rare, however, for the creation and nurturing of anything so complex as a singles program demands the fullest possible use of human and institutional resources. Questionnaires have been effective as a means of gauging interest in a singles program. I would recommend that the questionnaire be sent to all members of the church, so that nonsingles might indicate their approval and support of the proposal. There might also be room on the questionnaire for the recipient to suggest that single persons of their acquaintance be sent notice of the proposed program. Other conventional methods of circulating announcements, such as church bulletins, pulpit announcements, and newspaper releases are likely to bring responses from interested singles. Should it fit the church's philosophy, the pastor can also send notices to other churches, plus singles organizations such as Parents Without Partners and singles recreational clubs.

Although it is not generally a procedure practiced by other singles organizations, I would strongly recommend that the pastor or other person who is taking responsibility for developing the program meet each potential group attendee *individually* prior to the first meeting. By starting on a basis of conveying interest and concern for the single person *as a special person*, one will have taken a most important step toward creating an organization that shows a personal interest in the single person's psychological, practical, and spiritual needs. Every beginning group needs some cause and some person to form a temporary bond between the people present. Specialists in group dynamics stress the importance of a group leader's realizing that, in the beginning, a group of people is not really a group—they will continue to see themselves as individuals until that time when they begin to care about and identify with each other. For this reason the church representative must insure that the first participants relate to each other in an open, warm manner. The relationship that they form with each other will serve as the model for the singles program that will follow.

From the beginning, it should be clear that this is a *church* singles program—sponsored by the church, housed and funded by the church, administered by the church, and intended to function in a manner commensurate with the practices and purposes of that church. Unless this point is kept in mind, the singles program may not continue to reflect the church's plans for it. Single people are like any others in that there are those who are constructive and those who are destructive. Reverend Jim Smoke of the Garden Grove Community Church warns of three particularly "dangerous" kinds of singles: career singles, negative singles, and embittered formerly marrieds. When we are dealing with a population who number many who are lonely, embittered, ego-blemished and hungry for attention, it is likely that they will have a disproportionate effect unless measures are taken to prevent their controlling the group.

Most pastors are quite experienced in fostering and leading groups. Their parishioners usually are not. Good intentions and devoted service are not a substitute for expertise. If the pastor or one of his professional staff, or a professionally or experientially qualified parishioner are not available to serve as consultants, in liaison and as representatives of the church, then it would be wise for the pastor to consider bringing in an expert from the outside. This expert could be a professional specialist in group work, or a lay person experienced in such work. This kind of help may cost money initially, but it may well make the difference between a successful or an unsuccessful singles group program. If the pastor does not know himself to be an expert in singles' problems and group dynamics, then he should not hesitate to ask for help. There are many counselors, psychologists, social workers, and other group specialists whose desire to make new contacts may motivate their volunteering their services.

The "who" and the "how" of starting a church singles group are relatively easy to deal with. It is in the "why" that we begin to question the need, the wisdom, and the purposes of church singles groups.

WHY?

Psychologists believe that behavior is purposive; that is, goal-directed, and that, therefore, if one wants to know why a person or group is doing a certain thing, then the answer is to be found by determining what the goals or results of that behavior are. We know, too, that the rewards of a behavior can be both primary and secondary. For example, a man may work very hard (behavior) in order to make money (goal) so that he can live comfortably (reward). Money and comfortable living are primary rewards or gains deriving from working seventy hours a week. He may also be motivated (whether or not he is conscious of it) by a need to reduce anxiety or to overcome feelings of social inferiority. Going one step further, if we wish a person to learn and practice a particular behavior, all that is needed is for that person to aspire to a goal that can be attained by engaging in the required behavior. The goal, or gain, can be a primary or secondary one. So what? Well, if a church is deliberating about whether it will offer a singles program, the basic question is: "Why should we? What do we hope to accomplish? What are our goals?"

Obviously, unless a church can specify what the goals are that it hopes can be achieved through a singles program, then it should go no further. If, after this kind of self-questioning, the church can delineate its purposes or goals, then there is reason to move forward. A few of the possible goals which might be sought are:

> Offering emotional support and reassurance.
> Providing companionship and social contacts.
> Sponsoring social and recreational activities.
> Instilling attitudes of self-worth, optimism, and trust.
> Adding a sense of meaning and purpose to life.
> Instilling confidence and faith in organized religion.
> Teaching concepts of values, ethics, and morals.
> Making available various kinds of practical knowledge and assistance.
> Forming a relationship, even a commitment, to that church.
> Encouraging prayer, Bible study, and christian service.
> Educating parishioners about marriage, divorce, love, and the problem of single persons.

Broadening the scope of the church leaders' social
awareness.
Arranging for periods of spiritual contemplation,
discussion, and sharing.

If, then, a church should succeed in identifying what it
hopes to accomplish in a singles program, its next task will be
to determine what behaviors will enable the church and the
single persons to attain mutually acceptable and satisfying
goals. That is, the church must do certain things so that the
singles will do certain things—so that the goals can be
reached. It will also be important that both sides understand
(even though it may never be stated in concrete terms) that
the gains each seeks and receives will be of both the primary
and the secondary kinds.

In a sense, the church is in a selling position, and single
people are the buyers. Since the "product" or "package" is
the singles program, then the church needs to realistically
assess exactly what will "sell." In less commercial terms,
what can the proposed church singles program offer that the
single person needs and wants? The answers can be listed
under four major headings: Practical, Social, Psychological
and Spiritual.

Practical Needs of the Single Person

I have never been able to quite figure it out, or to verify it
from my own experience, but it seems an established fact that
single persons are not considered good risks by employers,
banks, landlords, credit card companies, and married people. Persons who have never been married have practical
problems that, although they may not be more severe than
those of married people, at least are different from those of
married people. Worse, and more specific to their single
state, are problems faced by divorced persons—especially
women—especially if they have children—especially if they
are inexperienced in meeting life alone. Ask a recently
divorced mother if she is having any problems adjusting to

her divorce, and she will either nod helplessly or engage you in a two-hour discourse. Rather than listing the practical problems faced by singles, I shall suggest some techniques by which a church singles group could be of significant service to single persons.

Financial problems, not just an insufficiency of money, are almost a given for divorced persons. Singles have questions, such as the following: "How do I go about finding out whether I am eligible for welfare or Medicare? Can I do anything about the fact that I was turned down for a credit card? Can I deduct the money I spend for child-care while I am working? Is there any way I can force my husband to keep up his alimony and/or child support payments? Do you know of any moderately priced apartment houses where they accept children? I am really having trouble with my budget; do you know where I could get some advice? Do you know where I can buy things at a discount? Can you advise me about installment buying? How can I keep from making some dumb mistakes when I buy a car? Is it possible for me to have my alimony payments to my wife reduced?" Many questions, but where to find the answers?

Employment also ranks as a concern for single persons, particularly those who have recently entered the employment market as a result of divorce, widowhood, moving away from home, military discharge, or changes in place of residence. Some people have no idea as to what types of jobs they are qualified to fill, what the pay scales and career possibilities are, which extra benefits to look for—such as overtime, vacation plans, medical insurance, life insurance, automatic or earned pay increases, job stability, and pension plans. More crucial than informational problems are the feelings of depression, guilt, self-doubt, self-consiousness, and pessimism, which often hinder the single person who suddenly finds him/herself in the job market. Very often, what is most needed is someone who can help the single person to deal with the psychological aspects of presenting him/herself to prospective employers.

Most divorced persons who have custody of their children

have similar problems in relation to their children. How does one handle all the manifold emotional and practical problems faced by the parent who has no spouse? The phenomenal growth of organizations such as Parents without Partners attests to the numbers of single parents seeking help with the problems that take place when a woman begins to react to her children's reactions to their parents' divorce.

Not only does the parent need help, but so do the children, for they, too, are nearly overwhelmed with the wave of changes being imposed on them. When will they see their dad? Where will they live, and will they have to give up having their own rooms? Will they make new friends and adjust to the new school? Since their mother now has to work, who will take care of them and what will they do all day? Should they find part-time jobs? Do our parents perceive how upset we kids are with them? And the mother, or father, have his or her own ambivalent feelings about "the children problem" been resolved? When people are divorced or widowed there is no more problematic or unsettling area than that having to do with children. The parents need help. The children need help. And the parents and children need help with each other.

As can be inferred from the discussions about problems related to finances, employment, and children, single persons have numerous problems that are related to legal considerations. Financially, the timing is bad; for by the time couples have divorced and suffered the attendant monetary losses, they have little money left over for legal consultation. Legal advice is also likely to be out of easy reach of many widows and young singles. Many of the legal problems people have are serious and complex to them even though a person with expertise at law would find it a simple matter to help solve the problems. As is so often true, a small contribution by one person can reap a large dividend for the recipient.

I believe that the church can make an important contribution toward bettering the lives of single persons by assisting them in resolving many of the practical problems that often crowd upon them. In so doing, it would do much to attract and retain them as members of its singles program. The plan is this: Every church has members who, because of their professional, experiential, and avocational backgrounds would be competent to serve as referral persons for specific problems. They would be able to handle many matters themselves, and would be able to refer the singles group member on to another person or agency when necessary. This consultation-referral service would be staffed by church members or other volunteers, who would be available for a few hours a week. The service would best be administered by someone with a background in social work or community referral service.

A church that is known to be interested in offering both spiritual and practical aid to single persons is very likely to attract many singles who would not be receptive to fulfilling their spiritual needs until their practical problems have been relieved. By fulfilling some specific needs, the church singles program will have created a new opportunity for achieving its goals.

Social Needs of the Single Person

Not all never-married persons are lonely or bored. Some of them prefer solitude. Others are happily enjoying the fruits of bachelorhood. But most of them, I believe, *are* lonely, and they often do feel restless and bored. There are many possible explanations as to why people might be socially inept or withdrawn. Whatever the reasons, the success of ski clubs, singles apartment complexes, dance studios, computer dating services, and singles bars attest to the social hunger that they are designed to satisfy. And social needs are the *only* needs that commercial singles programs care to satisfy.

Older people (I have hesitated to use that term ever since the time I gave a lecture to a Methodist church group and referred to "older people." A white-haired little lady shot to her feet and demanded, "Older than what?")—anyhow, people who are older often are lonely. Some are tragically neglected; rejected by their remaining family; dejected by their paltry prospects for a fuller life. Retired, widowed, perhaps short on funds and health, family gone, friends deceased, people from sixty on are ready, waiting for a way to reenter the world where things are happening and people are interacting.

The never-married and over-fifty singles have usually had time to adjust to their single status, which they may have chosen to retain. There are millions of other singles who are, to say the least, not enjoying the changes in their social life imposed by divorce or the death of a spouse. They are the people most likely to involve themselves in singles programs, for they are the ones most likely to be seeking an opportunity to reestablish themselves in social and interpersonal relationships. They want companionship and a social life, but their problems and their psychological state may differ greatly from those of the never-married. No matter whether or not they were relieved or grieved to be free of their former mate, they have suffered significant reactions to their reentry into a single life.

I have counseled hundreds of couples who were on the verge of divorce. Those who do divorce experience similar aftereffects. If one has not undergone a divorce, with its overtones of anger, anxiety, uncertainty, worry, depression and failure, and its undertones of quiet, doubt, pessimism, rejection, self-devaluation, and loneliness, will find it difficult to appreciate what the recently divorced person is feeling. Certainly, a divorce rarely does much to enhance one's self-image and self-confidence. One wants to be loved, but may feel unsure that one is lovable. One want someone to love, yet is not convinced that one will ever love again. One longs for companionship, but finds it difficult to even "be there" for another person. The newly single person wistfully recalls past times of pleasure in other people's company—wistful because many of those friends and companions are no longer part of their new life. One worries about the material and emotional effects on the children, clings to those children as ties to the past, solaces of the present and hope for the future, yet resents them as drains on one's already meager resources.

Feelings of quiet and selfdoubt incline one to withdraw from the competition of dating and socializing. Often there is a tiredness or lassitude that precludes doing anything more than just surviving. The feeling of being trapped in a marriage gives way to a feeling of being trapped in single life. Although you struggle to hold onto people whom you know and feel comfortable with, you know that you must make an effort to meet new people. Single now after years of married lif you yearn for physical contact, while trying to decide under what terms and with whom you might involve yourself.

Well, you are single and you are lonely, but where can you go to meet people? And what do you want when you do meet them? Nearly every newly divorced or widowed person I have known has run the gauntlet of blind dates, dating services, singles apartments, singles cruises, Sunday morning church services, political clubs, and bars. When they find themselves ignored or devalued by those whom they find there, they tend to become disheartened and to lose confidence. When they realize that they are not meeting the kind of people they are looking for, they begin to wonder whether they will have to choose between changing their standards or being alone. This decision period marks a point at which the single person is an especially good candidate for a church singles group.

We know that millions of single persons have an unfulfilled desire to do something for fun with somebody. A church that wishes to draw people into its realm of influence must—just as though it were a commercial operation—examine its product. Many successful enterprises offer what are called "leaders"; these are attractive features or bargains designed to entice customers onto the premises—where they are introduced to the product that the company hopes to sell. The church singles program's "leaders" are its social activities. Single persons have basically the same social and recreational interests as do married people—and they often have more time to devote to them.

It requires no special expertise to design a

social-recreational program, especially if the participants themselves share in or even lead the planning. The sample monthly schedule of social events offered by the Garden Grove Community Church, which I introduced earlier in this book, illustrates the wide range of get-togethers that a CSG can offer. Obviously, the larger the number of participants, the greater the diversity of activities that can be offered. If one church's singles group membership is small, it would do well to combine its social activities with that of one or more of its other church programs. A small membership means that the stimulation and possibilities of making new friends will be limited; and there may not be enough people interested to make it feasible for there to be special-interest activities, such as pool parties, square dancing, skiing, trips and outings to musical or athletic events.

Under the rubric of "social activities" would also fall lectures, study groups, workshops, work projects, and service-to-others projects. All provide singles members an opportunity to get together and to enjoy each other's company. To have fun does not always mean that one is playing. Humans are said to be social beings. We enjoy being in the company of other people. A successful CSG will realize that it must plan social interactions that offer a full range of the potentials. Social interaction is the behavior that leads to the emotional-psychological rewards that people seek. This same social interaction provides a setting in whcih the church can progress toward realizing its own goals. In a way, the church is like a parent who is saying, "I will help you to have fun, but I am more concerned with your psychological-spiritual development." This strategem is, of course, employed in the church's nonsingles programs. This is fine, perhaps necessary, but therein is often demonstrated a tactical error—or an invalid psychological premise—which is being capitalized upon by many of the more conservative churches. This error lies in some churches' belief that social concerns and social activities are the lures that will draw and bind people to the church. In contrast, I believe that for the church to accomplish its mission it must concentrate most of its energy toward meeting human needs in the following two dimensions: *psychological* and *spiritual.*

Psychological Needs of the Single Person

People everywhere, regardless of their mental state, are finding it costly to compete in today's society. Costly in terms of the strain and drain upon one's limited resources of emotional strengths. Those who have suffered the stresses of divorce, widowhood, or unwanted solitude differ only in that they may have no well to go to in order to refresh and replensih themselves. And, to have chosen singleness as a way of life does not mean that one's thirst for human interaction and intimacy has been abandoned or quaffed. A CSG can be of incalculable benefit to the single person, for who can calculate the quantity and quality of the individual demands for interaction, intimacy and intensity?

I do know that much of what people derive from their involvement in individual and group psychotherapy, growth groups, encounter groups, self-help books and all the myriad new types of self-improvement programs could better be served by the proper kind of church singles programs. In order to explain what I mean by "proper," I must first describe what I would like to see happen in CSGs. I am convinced that, by a process of self-selection, the people who are motivated to attend singles programs are the ones who are most amenable to the kind of psychological help I would like to see them receive. They may not be in greater need than those single persons who do not participate in organized singles activities, and they may not be aware of their receptiveness, but nevertheless they comprise a group of people who could benefit enormously from a CSG that addresses itself to the psychological dimension.

Some of the psychological needs that a CSG could meet are the needs for companionship, support, reassurance, warmth and affection, confrontation, self-understanding, an improved self-concept, freedom from deleterious and harmful events and situations of the past, improved ability to understand and relate to other people, catharsis, rectification of "punishable" or unattractive traits, clarification of attitudes and beliefs, expunging or expiation of guilt, to name only a few. All these things *could* happen in a CSG, but they rarely *do*. This failure to meet single people's psychological needs is caused by two factors, the second of which follows as a result of the first:

1. Miscalculation by the pastor and/or his staff as to their ability to operate within a psychological frame of reference. Seventeen years ago I began offering consultation services to ministers on a case conference basis. I was astonished and appalled on finding that most of them had had little or no training or course work in counseling. Those who had had a modicum of preparation for counseling were often the least prepared, for they did not know what they did not know. And, at that time, very few clergymen had themselves found out at first hand the benefits of a group experience led by a psychologically sophisticated leader. As I explained in *Treadmill to Heaven*,[1] a person cannot take people where the himself has not been or give them what he does not have. Whether or not they have much faith in the principles and techniques of psychotherapy, no pastor can deny that thousands of professional counselors have full caseloads and satisfied clients. Some churches, however, are led by ministers who have prepared themselves, academically and experientially, to minister to their parishioners' psychological needs. These churches are the ones most likely to offer a full range of services in their singles program. These programs do not worry me. Nor am I as concerned about those churches and programs that are blatantly disinterested in dealing directly with single people's emotional and interpersonal problems. Not surprisingly, the singles programs that are, psychologically speaking, potentially the least effective—or the most dangerous—are those that believe that barely trained leaders can deal effectively with psychological problems . . . which leads to the second factor.

2. I have witnessed many examples of group meetings that attempted to provide the kinds of experience that are usually

present in a therapy group. Usually, a token apology to professionalism is made by referring to the groups with a qualifying adjective such as discussion, rap, *agape*, study, sharing, fellowship, or growth. The people who serve in the place of group counselors are described ad facilitators or enablers. And my finding has been thta such disclaimers mean next to nothing. The church that includes such groups in its program usually provides some form of training for the group leaders. About all this hit-and-miss approach to training accomplishes is to delude the church staff, the group leaders, and the single people into believing that they are engaged in an activity that will do much good and little harm. My criticism is not just the chauvinistic carping of an infringed-upon professional. Nor am I exaggerating the extent or the seriousness of the problem. I have sat in as a member of such groups housed in some of our most sophisticated churches. In no church that operated a large singles program did I find the groups led by anyone other than lay people who had prepared for their task other than by participating in a few "leadership" classes or workshops. The gross mishandling of singles group members that I have witnessed does not lead me to recommend the discontinuance of such programs—only that pastors take more seriously the need for adequate training of group leaders. Seminars intended to teach such tings as "how to get a group going," "Ways of inspiring confidence," "Techniques of assuring interaction," or "How to be an effective listener" are not adequate to prepare lay people—no matter how dedicated—for leading groups in which people's emotional problems are dealt with.

I believe—I believe very strongly—that single people have a great need for psychological help; and that in great part this need could be met through participation in a church singles program. I think it imperative, however, that such groups be led only by people who have been adequately prepared for their role. This does not mean that all such activities must be led by a professional counselor. What it *does* mean is that a church singles group program should have one or more professionally qualified counselors available, and on a continuing basis. Training for leaders, facilitators, or enablers does not ever end; nor should their own personnel growth ever be divorced from their role as group leaders. In short, there is a strong correlation between the talent, emotional makeup, and expertise of the leader and the benefit that group members derive from his or her leadership.

Many churches have trained counselors and teachers of psychology in their membership. When they do not, a pastor will have to look elsewhere for experts to help him minister to people's psychological needs. I know from experience that many professional counselors would be willing to assist in training church group leaders for little or no financial reembursement. Nor would they be displeased by the opportunity to make contacts and enhance their professional reputations. The desideratum, of course, would be for the pastor to have extensive training in psychology and that he have on his staff one or more persons who have training in counseling—preferably pastoral counseling. The advantage of having such a minister or pastoral counselor direct the singles program leads us to the fourth dimension, in which it is possible for single persons and the church to meet.

Spiritual Needs of the Single Person

Humans have spiritual needs. Single persons are humans. Therefore, single persons have spiritual needs. Well, I'm glad that we got that settled, for I know that it would be innane for me to discourse on the subject of whether spiritual needs and problems are an intrinsic aspect of the human condition. What is, however, germane to the subject of this book is the question of what the church is doing specifically for single people. Sociologists, philosophers, theologians, and psychologists have described a condition variously as anomie, existential anxiety, spiritual impoverishment, the search for meaning, etc. If these terms are appropriate diagnostic labels for today's "human condition," then we cannot deny that single persons are prime targets for a church program that aims to ameliorate the confusion, disenchantment, and emptyness characteristic of a person who has recently had reason to doubt that anything or anyone can be believed in.

Psychologists know that often the person who is feeling the most anxiety, despair, skepticism, loneliness, and sense of hopelessness and meaninglessness is the very person who may be the most receptive to the promise of hope and meaning. It is hard enough nowadays to keep your sense of values and purpose in life. All around us there is the cry of "the new morality." God is said to be dead and true meaning—the only meaning—is to be found in accepting responsibility for getting in touch with your true being in an authentic manner, humanistically centered in the existential reality of what is. I'm not sure what all that means, except that if I concern myself very much with my spiritual life, then I am probably copping out on taking responsibility for my life. Of course, I could meditate in a transcendental way, get EST-ed or find out what my body is trying to tell me. If I am single, every day's television programs, movies, newspapers, magazines and even many pulpits and podiums recommend—demand— that I get in touch with today's reality. A recent article devoted to the contemporary single woman explained that:

> Unlike her 1960s sister, who still tended to trade sexual intimacy for emotional commitment from a man, the 1970s single girl doesn't necessarily require that a sexual relationship be meaningful. Many women today are sleeping with one or several men they like, but have no intention of living with or marrying. Frequently such women are involved with their careers; though they expect to marry someday, marriage is not an immediate goal. Meanwhile, they combat loneliness by building solid, supportive relationships with women. Nor does the "new breed" of single girl consider herself "promiscuous." Formerly looked upon as any extramarital sexual activity, the new definition of promiscuity is: sex that's repetitive, joyless, impersonal, empty. The consensus today is sex that's pleasurable for both partners is good in itself.[2]

There is some reason to believe that spiritual guidance and involvement are needed in today's society. In my book, *Let Me Live!,*[3] I proposed a theory that true maturity could be attained only by, and when, a person has symbolically become his/her own parent. The more I observe what are the standards, values, and ego ideals being promulgated today, the more I am convinced that people are aspiring to become their own children. Children, who normally are hedonistic and self-centered, are not usually committed to anyone or anything—other than avoiding pain and seeking pleasure. Today people are relatively free of the religious, social, legal, economic, and psychological sanctions that previously limited the kinds of behavior one could safely practice. We are free *from*, but are having trouble with, our freedom *to*. This is expecially true of the divorced single person who has been "freed" from the restrictions imposed upon the married person who lives a life whose commitments limit his/her range of "acceptable" behavior.

A large proportion of divorced, widowed, or never-married people have gone through the same cycle in regard to their value system and their behavior: suppression, liberation, indulgence, satiation, disenchantment, uncertainty, and a search for meaning. Some remain fixated at that point in their own personal maze; some scurry into one blind alley after another only to return to their starting point; some— and there are many of them—become receptive to guidance and assistance. It is these single persons who are ready, even hungry, to taste of the fruits of church involvement.

No pastor or faithful church member needs to be lectured to on what the church can give single seekers. The same church activities that the married person finds pleasurable and helpful also are rewarding to the single person. Marital status has little to do with the capacity to benefit from prayer, singing, sermons, lectures, Bible study, discussion groups, communion, testimony, tithing, counseling, and service to others. And yet, many church singles groups create programs that are almost unrelated to the principles and practices of that church. Although some of them make a token acknowledgment that this is a *church* singles group by singing a few hymns before the "real" activities take place, and then close with a prayer as though to remind everyone that all the evening's activities have something to do with church, they really seem afraid of offending or scaring off the singles members if the program becomes too "churchy." Well, I agree that we don't want to drive away the prospective member by trying to impose on him/her a commitment or belief system for which they are not ready, but I don't think that we have to apologize for being a church which is intended to share the Gospel and change lives!

In chapter 7 I described a church-integrated singles program. What made this program effective was not the relative emphasis or deemphasis of explicitly religious activities. Rather, it was the observable fact that in this group there was manifest the devotion to love, trust, acceptance, self-understanding, interest in others, religious values, Christian commitment, enjoyment of the other person, sharing of self, and spiritual development that are the purpose and proof of the Gospel. A key factor in this CISG's value was the church staff member who led the group. It is not only that his intelligence, personality, motivation, character, or expertise would mark him as above average. No, I believe that one particular quality set him above most singles group leaders whom I have met and observed: He was knowledgeable and trained in understanding, interacting with, and leading others in an effort intended to be of benefit to them. This is not to say that every church staff member who leads programs or groups must be a counselor. But, from my admittedly biased position, it does mean that—all other things being equal—the singles group leader who has been trained to work intimately with people will be the one who is the most successful.

I have attended singles groups, and subgroups, where I was horrified by the clumsiness and ineffectiveness of the "leader." Most such churches make an effort to provide some training for its singles group leaders. Unfortunately, these training programs are usually led by church staff members, who themselves are marginally qualified to lead a group. Or they call in some "expert," who presents an alluring array of techniques for leading groups. Many church singles group leaders, I believe, prove the truth of the adage that "a little learning is a dangerous thing."

Allowing a group leader to function without benefit of academic preparation, practical supervision or searching self-study is not excused or made less potentially pernicious, and is not justified by the ploy of referring to the group as "only" a rap group, discussion group, sharing group, or fellowship group, or describing the person in charge as an enabler or facilitator—to light-touch such activity is dangerous. Over a period of four years I trained 200 college undergraduates to co-lead therapy groups. They were effective, and they were professional. Likewise, I have trained drug addicts, housewives, alcoholics, ex-convicts and teenagers to function effectively and safely as leaders in groups that were intended to be therapeutic. Staff members and volunteers could be trained to conduct group experiences that would be of psychological, practical, and spiritual benefit to single persons. And there are very few churches that could not make it possible for its singles group leaders to have the needed training. It should be obvious that people will not return to a group led by people they do not trust.

I am not asking that church singles group leaders become professional psychotherapists. What I am asking is that they recognize that they are dealing with complex human beings, whose emotions and psyches may be especially vulnerable to assault or mishandling, and that these leaders respect the need to better prepare themselves for this sensitive and important work.

Since some churches treat their singles program like a distant relative, it is possible for the pastor and the parishioners not to be intimately involved in their singles program. They then run the risk of being beguiled by growth statistics and secondhand evaluations of the program. Some people in the church, not just the staff people directly involved, should be functionally involved in the singles program. Otherwise the church will find it difficult or even impossible to accurately assess the extent to which the church's principles and purposes are being successfully met in the singles program. This is necessary even when the preponderance of the singles group's activities are what might be termed "social" or "religious." We are still dealing with human beings, and they deserve the best.

If the church staff members who are responsible for the singles program are psychologically sophisticated, and if they have insight into their own psychological dynamics, they will not only be well prepared to lead and to supervise, but they will also be able to identify those singles group members, and especially leaders, whose personalities, characters, or goals would be in opposition to the church's purposes. As an additional safeguard, most churches require that some of the officers and leaders of the singles program be members of that church. This is wise for, like any other sample of the population, some potential singles members and leaders would be counterproductive to the group and to the church.

In short, if a church singles group is to be of spiritual benefit to the participants, then their coming together must be a *spiritual* experience.

SUMMARY:

A Singular Opportunity

When I had finished my internship and received my Ph.D., I opened my own office, hung out my shingle, and waited for patients who never came. In addition to making me very hungry, it made me very sad. After all, I was well trained, available, and sincerely wanted to offer what I knew to be a needed service. So I made the rounds of potential referral sources, addressed service clubs, volunteered consulting services at probation offices, accepted nonpaying patients, and still I felt frustrated because I was able to touch so few people. Twelve years later, I began training and counseling clergymen. It was then that I came to appreciate the position of a clergyman who must often wait for people to come to him so that they can find what they were looking for. He knows also that many people who need what his church has to offer will never appear at his church, and of those with whom he does come in contact, many will have special needs that his church program is not designed to meet. Among these people are single persons.

Because married people, and the institutions that they dominate, hold certain prejudices toward the unmarried, even when single persons are not being perceived and dealt with on the basis of stereotypes, they often find that they just do not fit easily into situations where all but a few of the other participants are married. At a stage of their life where they are in the greatest need of fellowship, support, assistance, and spiritual nurturing, there seems nowhere they can go. Some churches have led the way in creating singles programs.

Church singles programs range from the laissez-faire type, which I have labeled as "church-sponsored," to the "church-related," the "church-integrated," and the "church-dominated." Without question, my observations and analyses show the church-integrated group to be the optimal design. This type of church-singles interaction is uniquely capable of putting the church and its singles group members in a mutually satisfying relationship.

If there is one factor that determines the ultimate success or failure of a church singles group it is the leadership. By "leadership" I am referring not only to the pastor and the church staff members but also, particularly, to those persons whose leadership role places them in direct contact with the singles group members. No matter what the structure of the program, or the format of the meetings, what is most important is what happens between individuals in all their emotional, psychological and spiritual potential. These leaders need not be outstanding in any ways other than that they possess the kinds of character, personality, and spiritual development that will enable them to personify what that church represents. In order for them to be a positive influence on the single persons for whom they are responsible, these leaders must be trained in interpersonal skills.

Each of us is multifaceted, living many roles. The psychologist, the single person, the divorced person, the married person, the Christian—all of me feel and know the need for more church-integrated singles groups. Should you choose to become involved in such work, you will find that it is not easy, but you will know that what you are doing is important and it is good.

Notes

CHAPTER 1

1. *Los Angeles Times*, August 12, 1976.
2. Lynn Caine, *Widow*, (New York: Morrow, 1974).
3. Otis Young, "A Church Ministering to Singles," *The Christian Ministry*, March 1976, p. 8.
4. Morgan Simmons, "Our Ministry to Singles," *The Christian Ministry*, March 1976, p. 9.
5. Ibid., p. 9.
6. Young, p. 8.
7. Richard Chen, *Newsweek*, June 12, 1972, p. 73.
8. Britton Wood, "The Single Adult: the Church's New Frontier," *Evangelical Newsletter*, vol. 3, no. 15, May 1976.
9. Elmer Towns, *The Church and The Single Adult* (Glendale, Calif.: Regal Books, 1967), p. 5.
10. Robert S. Ellwood, Jr., *One Way—The Jesus Movement and Its Meaning* (Englewood Cliffs, N.J.: Prentice-Hall, 1973).
11. Sarah Jepson, *For the Love of Singles*, (Carol Stream, Ill.: Creation House, 1970), pp. 75–76.

CHAPTER 2

1. Olive Evans, "When Singles Bars Fail: Some Alternatives," *New York Times*, May 12, 1976.
2. Jacelyn Paine, "They Want to Be Alone," *Los Angeles Times*, August 12, 1976.
3. Jepson, p. 61.
4. Ibid., p. 63.

5. I Cor. 7:32. *The Oxford Annotated Bible*, Revised Standard Version (New York: Oxford University Press, 1962).

6. John Fischer, lecture at Peninsula Bible Church of Palo Alto, Calif.

7. William Lyon, *First Mother, Now You*(Newport Beach, Calif.: Quail Street Publishing Company, 1977).

CHAPTER 3

1. Bretton Wood, "The Single Adult: The Church's New Frontier," *Theology, News and Notes*, March 1976; referred to in *The Evangelical Newsletter*, vol. 3, no. 15, May 1976.

2. Jim Smoke, "Directions in Single Adult Ministries," pamphlet published by the Garden Grove Community Church, Garden Grove, Calif., 1976.

3. Marshall Bryant Hodge, *Your Fear of Love* (Garden City, N.Y.: Doubleday, Dolphin, 1967), p. 186.

4. Ibid, pp. 187–188.

5. Stephen Clark, *Building Christian Communities*. (Notre Dame: Ave Maria Press, 1972), p. 70.

6. Michael Scanlon, *Inner Healing* (New York: Paulist Press, 1974), p. 65.

7. Meyer Friedman and Ray H. Roseman, *Type A Behavior and Your Heart*, (Greenwich, Connecticut: Fawcett Crest, 1975), p. 91.

8. Robert S. Ellwood, Jr., *The Jesus Movement and Its Meaning*, (Englewood Cliffs, N.J.: Prentice-Hall, 1973), p. 55.

9. Michael A. Hamilton (Ed.), *The Charismatic Movement* (Grand Rapids: William Eerdmans Publishing Co., 1975), p. 8.

10. Abraham Maslow, *Religions, Values, and Peak Experiences* (New York: The Viking Press, 1964).

11. Adelaide Bry, *EST—Sixty Hours that Can Change Your Life*, (New York: Avon Books, 1976), p. 108.

12. Ibid, p. 57.

13. Wesley C. Baker, *The Split-Level Fellowship* (New York: Westminster Press), p. 39.

14. Marvin Mayers, *Journal of the American Scientific Affiliation*, Sept. 1971, p. 92.

CHAPTER 4

1. "Church for Singles," *Newsweek*, June 12, 1972, p. 73.

2. New York Times, May 12, 1976.

3. Ibid.

4. Ibid.

5. Dean M. Kelley, *Why Conservative Churches Are Growing* (New York: Harper & Row, 1972), p. 37.

CHAPTER 5

1. Kelly, p. 101.

2. Kelly, pp. 13–14.

3. Ashley Montagu, *Man in Process* (New York: Mentor Books, 1961), p. 25.

4. Wesley C. Baker, *The Split-Level Fellowship* (Philadelphia: Westminster Press, 1965).

CHAPTER 6

1. Kelley, p. 10.

2. Bill Beatty, an interview in *The Tidings*, Los Angeles, June 25, 1976.

CHAPTER 7

1. Janet Fix, "We Need a Family," *Christian Life*, 1976, pp. 54–64.

CHAPTER 8

1. Lyon.

2. Ada Lum, *Single & Human* Downers Grove, Ill.: InterVarsity Press, 1976).

3. Towns.

CHAPTER 9

1. William Lyon, *Treadmill to Heaven* (Newport Beach, Calif.: Quail Street Publishing Company, 1976).

2. William Appleton, "Living Single in the Seventies," *Cosmopolitan*, July 1976, p. 155.

3. William Lyon, *Let Me Live! (North Quincy, Mass.: Christopher Publishing House, 1976), chap. 2.